G000299696

gluten-free

breakfast • starters & snacks
main courses • sides • desserts

mc
rae
PUBLISHING

mc rae PUBLISHING

This book was conceived, edited and designed by McRae Publishing Ltd London

Copyright © 2015 McRae Publishing Ltd

All rights reserved. Unauthorized reproduction, in any manner, is prohibited.

www.mcraepublishing.com

Culinary Notebooks series

Project Director Anne McRae
Art Director Marco Nardi

GLUTEN-FREE
Photography Brent Parker Jones
Text Carla Bardi
Editing Christine Price, Daphne Trotter
Food Styling Lee Blaylock
Food Preparation and Assistant Stylists
Mark Hockenhull, Milli Lee
Layouts Aurora Granata

ISBN 978-1-910122-20-4

Printed in China

contents

getting started

Here you will find more than 100 gluten-free recipes for every occasion. To help you choose the right one, we have rated them for difficulty: 1 (simple), 2 (fairly simple), or 3 (challenging). In these two pages we have highlighted 25 of the most enticing dishes, just to get you started!

● QUICK

AVOCADO & BLUE CHEESE
salads

SPINACH & BLUEBERRY
smoothies

ASIAN GREENS
with oyster sauce

FRESH FRUIT
with vermouth

APPLE crisp

CRANBERRY
BREAKFAST
cookies

SUN-DRIED TOMATO
loaf

● EASY

VEGETABLES
al cartoccio

EASY ICE CREAM cake

SEEDY CRACKERS with hummus

HOT CHOICE

STRAWBERRY & PINEAPPLE
smoothies

ALMOND BREAKFAST
cake

MINI CHILI BEEF
pies

CHOCOLATE CARAMEL
macarons

CHOCOLATE PECAN
torte

GLUTEN-FREE
granola

ROSEMARY crackers

EDITOR'S CHOICE

GLUTEN-FREE pizza

CURRIED CHICKEN
& VEGETABLE pie

GLUTEN-FREE
citrus torte

BEST BREAKFAST

GLUTEN-FREE
pancakes

BEST SNACK

CHEESE straws

BEST MAIN COURSE

GLUTEN-FREE QUICHE
with mushrooms & goat
cheese

BEST SIDE DISH

GARLIC mash

BEST DESSERT

LEMON
cheesecake

breakfast

GLUTEN-FREE pancakes

1³/₄ cups (270 g) sorghum flour
¹/₄ cup (30 g) buckwheat flour
¹/₃ cup (30 g) almond flour
¹/₄ cup (30 g) potato starch or tapioca starch
1¹/₂ teaspoons baking powder
³/₄ teaspoon sea salt flakes
³/₄ teaspoon xanthan gum
1 cup (250 ml) milk
1 cup (250 ml) water
2 large eggs, lightly beaten
¹/₄ cup (60 ml) coconut oil
1 tablespoon honey or raw agave nectar
1 teaspoon vanilla extract (essence)
¹/₂ teaspoon almond extract (essence)
1-2 tablespoons butter or vegetable oil, to grease
Maple syrup, warmed, or chopped fresh fruit or preserves (jam), to serve
Confectioners' (icing) sugar, to dust

Serves 4-6 • Preparation 15 minutes • Cooking 15-20 minutes
Difficulty 1

1. Combine the sorghum flour, buckwheat flour, almond flour, potato starch, baking powder, salt, and xanthan gum in a bowl, mixing well. Make a well in the center and pour in the milk, water, eggs, coconut oil, honey, vanilla, and almond extract. Beat with a whisk until silky and smooth.

2. Lightly grease a pancake skillet or small crêpe pan with a little of the butter or oil and place over medium-high heat.

3. Test the pan by shaking a drop of water onto it. If it pops and sizzles, it is hot enough.

4. Using a ladle, pour a scoop of the batter into the heated pan. When tiny bubbles have formed on top, carefully flip the pancake with a spatula. Cook until firm, 2-3 minutes. Repeat with the remaining batter.

5. Serve as soon as possible with warm maple syrup, fresh fruit, or fruit preserves.

If you liked this recipe, you will love these as well.

CRANBERRY
& COCONUT
flapjacks

CRANBERRY
BREAKFAST cookies

ALMOND BREAKFAST
cake

SPINACH & BLUEBERRY smoothies

2 cups (300 g) fresh blueberries
1 cup (50 g) fresh spinach leaves
1 cup (250 ml) plain yogurt
$^1/_2$ cup (120 ml) milk
1 tablespoon honey

Serves 2 • Preparation 10 minutes • Difficulty 1

1. Place two glasses in the freezer to chill. Reserve a few whole blueberries to garnish.
2. Combine the remaining blueberries, spinach, yogurt, milk, and honey in a blender and blend until smooth.
3. Pour into the glasses, sprinkle the reserved blueberries on top, and serve.

STRAWBERRY & PINEAPPLE smoothies

2   cups (500 ml) plain yogurt
12   strawberries + 4 extra, to garnish
2   cups fresh pineapple, tough core removed, chopped
2   medium bananas
2   teaspoons vanilla extract (essence)
8   ice cubes

Serves 4 • Preparation 10 minutes • Difficulty 1

1. Place four glasses in the freezer to chill. Place the four extra strawberries in the freezer to chill as well.

2. Combine the yogurt, 12 strawberries, pineapple, bananas, vanilla, and ice cubes in a blender and blend until smooth.

3. Pour into the glasses, garnish with the chilled strawberries, and serve.

Oats are gluten-free, however you must make sure that the package is marked gluten-free as many oats are prepared or stored with products containing gluten and can become "contaminated." Furthermore, if serving oats to people with celiac disease, remember that oats contain a protein called avenin and a small percentage of celiacs will also react to it. Most celiacs can safely eat oats, but not everyone. If you are unsure about serving oats, replace them in this recipe with one cup each of ground flaxseed, rice bran, quinoa flakes, and chia seeds.

This granola can be stored in an airtight container for up to two weeks.

GLUTEN-FREE granola

4	cups (400 g) gluten-free rolled oats
2	cups (250 g) mixed nuts and seeds (chopped almonds, pecans, walnuts, black and white sesame seeds, poppy seeds, chia seeds, and flaxseeds)
1	cup (70 g) unsweetened coconut flakes
$\frac{1}{2}$	cup (120 ml) apple juice
$\frac{1}{2}$	cup (120 ml) liquid honey
$\frac{1}{4}$	cup (60 ml) coconut oil
1	tablespoon vanilla extract (essence)
$\frac{1}{2}$	teaspoon ground cinnamon
1	teaspoon sea salt flakes
2	cups (250 g) mixed dried unsweetened fruit (dried cranberries, apricots, apples, pineapple, golden raisins/ sultanas, etc.)

Makes 12–15 servings • Preparation 15 minutes • Cooking 25–35 minutes Difficulty 1

1. Preheat the oven to 325°F (160°C/gas 3).

2. Combine the oats, nuts, seeds, and coconut flakes in a large bowl.

3. Combine the apple juice, honey, coconut oil, vanilla extract, cinnamon, and salt in a medium saucepan. Gently heat until the salt is dissolved and coconut oil is liquid.

4. Pour the apple juice mixture over the oats mixture and toss to coat. Spread the mixture evenly on a baking sheet. Bake for 25–35 minutes, until golden. Stir the mixture every 10–15 minutes to make sure it bakes evenly.

5. Let the granola cool completely. It will become crunchier as it sits. Stir in the dried fruit when completely cool.

6. Serve with yogurt or milk and fresh fruit.

If you liked this recipe, you will love these as well.

SEED & NUT
breakfast bars

CRANBERRY & COCONUT
flapjacks

ALMOND BREAKFAST
cake

SEED & NUT breakfast bars

¹/₃	cup (90 g) butter, softened
¹/₃	cup (90 ml) honey
¹/₂	cup (100 g) raw sugar (Demerara or Barbados)
¹/₂	cup (50 g) rice bran
1	cup (100 g) quinoa flakes
¹/₂	cup (60 g) coarsely chopped walnuts
¹/₂	cup (60 g) raisins
2	tablespoons pumpkin seeds
2	tablespoons sunflower seeds
2	tablespoons sesame seeds
2	tablespoons shredded (desiccated) coconut
1	teaspoon ground cinnamon
¹/₄	teaspoon salt

Makes 12–16 bars • Preparation 15 minutes • Cooking 25–30 minutes
Difficulty 1

1. Preheat the oven to 375°F (190°C/gas 5). Butter a 7 x 11-inch (18 x 28-cm) baking pan.

2. Melt the butter with the honey and raw sugar in a medium saucepan over low heat, stirring constantly. Bring to a boil then simmer until the sugar has dissolved completely.

3. Remove from the heat and stir in the rice bran, quinoa flakes, walnuts, raisins, pumpkin seeds, sunflower seeds, sesame seeds, coconut, cinnamon, and salt.

4. Spoon the mixture evenly into the prepared pan, smoothing with the back of the spoon.

5. Bake for 25–30 minutes, until just golden.

6. Let cool completely in the pan before cutting into bars.

CRANBERRY & COCONUT flapjacks

2   tablespoons light corn (golden) syrup

$1/4$ cup (60 ml) honey

$2/3$ cup (150 g) salted butter

1   cup (150 g) old-fashioned oats (or $1/2$ cup each rice bran and quinoa flakes)

$2/3$ cup (100 g) unsweetened shredded (dessicated) coconut

$2/3$ cup (100 g) dried cranberries

Makes 12–16 squares • Preparation 15 minutes • Cooking 25–30 minutes
Difficulty 1

1. Preheat the oven to 350°F (180°C/gas 4). Lightly grease a 9-inch (23-cm) square baking pan.

2. Melt the corn syrup, honey, and butter in a medium saucepan over low heat, stirring until well combined. Remove the pan from the heat and stir in the oats, coconut, and cranberries.

3. Pour the flapjack mixture into the prepared baking pan, pressing it down gently into the corners of the pan.

4. Bake for 25–30 minutes, until golden brown.

5. Score the flapjack into pieces while still hot. Let cool completely in the pan before turning out. Slice and serve.

Oats contain a type of soluble fiber known as beta-glucan which has proven beneficial effects on cholesterol levels. Consuming just three grams of soluble oat fiber per day (about one bowl of oatmeal) typically lowers total cholesterol by 8–23 percent.

One again, remember that a very small number of celiacs are sensitive to oats; check with your medical advisor if you have any doubts.

BREAKFAST oatmeal

1 cup (250 ml) whole milk
1 cup (250 ml) water
$^1/_2$ teaspoon sea salt flakes
1 teaspoon vanilla extract (essence)
1 cup (100 g) gluten-free whole rolled oats
Maple syrup, to serve
Fresh sliced fruit or berries, to serve

Serves 2 • Preparation 15 minutes + 5 minutes to cool • Cooking 15–20 minutes • Difficulty 1

1. Combine the milk and water in a heavy-based saucepan over medium-high heat. Add the salt and vanilla and bring to a boil.

2. Pour in the oats, stirring vigorously with a wooden spoon. When the water returns to a boil, decrease the heat to low. Simmer, stirring every few minutes, until the oats are creamy and plump, 10–15 minutes.

3. Turn off the heat and cover the pan. Let the oatmeal sit for 5 minutes to fully absorb the liquid.

4. Pour into serving dishes and serve hot with maple syrup and fresh fruit of your choice.

If you liked this recipe, you will love these as well.

GLUTEN-FREE
pancakes

GLUTEN-FREE
granola

POLENTA
cake

POTATO & EGG pan-fry

Serves 4 • Preparation 15 minutes • Cooking 12 minutes
Difficulty 1

2	potatoes, halved and thinly sliced	1	tablespoon finely chopped fresh parsley
2	tablespoons extra-virgin olive oil		Freshly ground sea salt and black pepper
4	scallions (spring onions), thinly sliced	4	large eggs
2	tomatoes, coarsely chopped	1	cup (120 g) freshly grated Parmesan cheese

1. Sauté the potatoes in the oil in a large frying pan over medium heat until almost tender, about 5 minutes.

2. Add the scallions and tomatoes. Sauté until softened, about 2 minutes. Stir in the parsley and season with salt and pepper. Break the eggs gently over the mixture and sprinkle with the Parmesan. Decrease the heat to low.

3. Cover and simmer until the eggs have just set, about 5 minutes.

4. Cut into quarters, and serve hot.

BACON & EGG pies

Serves 6 • Preparation 15 minutes • Cooking 20–25 minutes
Difficulty 1

2	leeks, thinly sliced	1/2	cup (120 ml) light (single) cream
8	ounces (250 g) bacon slices, chopped	1	tablespoon whole-grain mustard
2	tablespoons extra-virgin olive oil		Freshly ground sea salt and black pepper
10	large eggs		

1. Preheat the oven to 350°F (180°C/gas 4). Grease six 3/4-cup (180-ml) ramekins with oil.

2. Sauté the leeks and bacon in the oil in a large frying pan over medium-high heat until the leeks have softened, about 3 minutes. Let cool slightly.

3. Meanwhile, beat 4 eggs with the cream and mustard in a medium bowl. Season with salt and pepper. Stir in the leek mixture. Mix well.

4. Spoon the mixture into the prepared ramekins. Crack one egg into each ramekin.

5. Bake for 15–20 minutes, until golden and set. Let cool in the ramekins for 5 minutes. Turn out onto racks. Serve at once.

FRITTATA with cream cheese

Serves 4 • Preparation 10 minutes • Cooking 10–15 minutes
Difficulty 1

2/3	cup (150 ml) cream cheese, softened		Freshly ground sea salt and black pepper
1/2	cup (60 g) freshly grated Parmesan	1/2	cup (60 g) freshly grated Gruyère
1/2	clove garlic, minced	1	tablespoon finely chopped fresh thyme
2	tablespoons basil		
1/2	teaspoon Worcestershire sauce	1/2	teaspoon dried marjoram
6	large eggs	1/4	cup (60 ml) extra-virgin olive oil
2	tablespoons milk		

1. Beat the cream cheese, Parmesan, garlic, basil, and Worcestershire sauce in a small bowl. Beat the eggs and milk in a large bowl. Season with salt and pepper. Stir in the Gruyère, thyme, and marjoram.

2. Heat half the oil in a large frying pan over medium heat. Pour in half the beaten eggs. Shake the pan with a rotating movement to spread. Cook until nicely browned on the underside. Transfer the frittata to a serving plate and keep warm.

3. Add the remaining oil to the pan. Pour the remaining egg mixture into the pan and cook as above.

4. Spread the cream cheese mixture over the first frittata. Top with the second frittata. Serve hot.

EGGS with broccoli & pancetta

Serves 2 • Preparation 15 minutes • Cooking 12–15 minutes
Difficulty 1

8	ounces (250 g) broccoli, cut into florets		and black pepper
		1/2	cup (60 g) diced pancetta or bacon
4	large eggs, lightly beaten	1	clove garlic, finely chopped
1/2	cup (60 g) freshly grated Parmesan cheese	2	tablespoons extra-virgin olive oil
	Freshly ground sea salt		

1. Cook the broccoli in a large pot of salted, boiling water until just tender, 6–8 minutes. Drain well and set aside.

2. Beat the eggs and cheese in a large bowl. Season with salt and pepper.

3. Sauté the pancetta and garlic in the oil in a large frying pan over medium heat until the garlic turns pale gold, about 1 minute. Add the broccoli and mix well.

4. Pour in the egg mixture. Cook over low heat for about 5 minutes, stirring often, until the eggs form large chunks. Serve hot.

To vary this recipe, replace the dried cranberries with the same amount of raisins or chopped candied peel or ginger.

CRANBERRY BREAKFAST cookies

½ cup (120 ml) chilled coconut milk

1 teaspoon freshly squeezed lemon juice

1 cup (150 g) brown rice flour

1 cup (100 g) gluten-free rolled oats

⅓ cup (50 g) quinoa flour

⅓ cup (50 g) tapioca flour

½ cup (100 g) firmly packed light brown sugar

1 tablespoon baking powder

½ teaspoon baking soda (bicarbonate of soda)

½ teaspoon sea salt flakes

Finely grated zest of 1 unwaxed orange

⅔ cup (150 g) unsalted butter, chilled

2 large eggs

1 cup (120 g) dried cranberries

2 tablespoons raw sugar, to sprinkle

Makes about 12 • Preparation 15 minutes • Cooking 18–20 minutes
Difficulty 1

1. Preheat the oven to 400°F (200°C/gas 6). Line a large baking sheet with parchment paper. Mix the coconut milk and lemon juice in a bowl and chill for 5 minutes.

2. Combine the brown rice flour, rolled oats, quinoa flour, tapioca flour, brown sugar, baking powder, baking soda, salt, and orange zest in a bowl, mixing well. Cut in the butter until the mixture resembles coarse crumbs.

3. Whisk 1 egg into the coconut milk mixture. Stir into the butter mixture with the cranberries. Press into a ball.

4. Roll out to about $^3/_4$ inch (2 cm) thick. Use a 2-inch (5-cm) round cookie cutter to cut out cookies. Place on the prepared baking sheet. Whisk the remaining egg and brush the tops of the cookies. Sprinkle with the raw sugar.

5. Bake for 18–20 minutes, until golden brown. Serve warm or at room temperature.

If you liked this recipe, you will love these as well.

HAZELNUT & ALMOND
cookies

POLENTA
cake

ALMOND BREAKFAST
cake

HAZELNUT & ALMOND cookies

3	tablespoons cornstarch (cornflour)
2	cups (200 g) finely ground hazelnuts
1	cup (100 g) finely ground almonds
1/4	teaspoon sea salt flakes
1	large egg, lightly beaten
1/2	cup (120 ml) freshly squeezed orange juice
1	tablespoon finely grated unwaxed orange zest
1 1/2	tablespoons maple or corn (golden) syrup
3	tablespoons apricot preserves
2	tablespoons finely chopped pistachios

Makes about 30 cookies • Preparation 30 minutes • Cooking 12–15 minutes • Difficulty 2

1. Preheat the oven to 300°F (150°C/gas 2). Line two large cookie sheets with parchment paper.

2. Mix the cornstarch, hazelnuts, almonds, and salt in a large bowl. Stir in the egg, orange juice, orange zest, and 1 tablespoon of maple syrup to form a soft, smooth dough.

3. Fit a pastry bag with a plain 1-inch (2.5-cm) tip. Spoon the mixture into the pastry bag and squeeze out half moons and wreaths on the prepared cookie sheets, spacing about 2 inches (5 cm) apart.

4. Bake for 12–15 minutes, until lightly golden. Transfer to racks to cool.

5. Warm the preserves in a small pan over low heat. Brush over the warm cookies and sprinkle with the pistachios.

POLENTA cake

½ cup (60 g) coarsely chopped blanched almonds
½ cup (50 g) chopped candied peel
¼ cup (60 ml) grappa or rum
3 tablespoons golden raisins (sultanas)
2 tablespoons chopped dried figs
4 cups (1 liter) milk
2½ cups (375 g) polenta (yellow cornmeal)
⅓ cup (50 g) rice flour
½ cup (100 g) sugar
⅔ cup (150 g) unsalted butter
½ teaspoon sea salt flakes

Serves 10–12 • Preparation 30 minutes • Cooking 1¼–1½ hours
Difficulty 2

1. Preheat the oven to 350°F (180°C/gas 4). Butter and flour a 10-inch (25-cm) springform pan.

2. Stir the almonds, candied peel, grappa, golden raisins, and figs in a medium bowl. Let stand for 15 minutes.

3. Bring the milk to a boil in a large saucepan over medium heat. Reduce the heat to low. Gradually add the polenta and rice flour, stirring constantly for 15 minutes. Stir in the sugar, butter, and salt, and cook, stirring occasionally, for 10 minutes.

4. Remove from the heat. Stir in the fruit and grappa mixture. Spoon the batter into the prepared pan.

5. Bake for 50–60 minutes, until lightly browned. After 30 minutes, cover the top of the cake loosely with a piece of aluminum foil to prevent it from drying out.

6. Cool the cake completely in the pan on a rack. Loosen and remove the pan sides to serve.

This cake is made with finely ground almond meal. Almond meal differs from almond flour in that it is almost always made by grinding the almonds with their skins so that you see flecks of skin in the meal. Almond flour is made from blanched almonds without their skins and is a plain white color.

This attractive cake goes beautifully with tea or coffee at breakfast or brunch, or any other time of the day!

ALMOND BREAKFAST cake

4	large eggs
2	tablespoons finely grated unwaxed lemon zest
$1/2$	teaspoon ground cinnamon
$1/4$	teaspoon ground cardamom
$1/2$	cup (100 g) sugar
$1^3/4$	cups (175 g) finely ground almond meal
1	teaspoon baking powder
$1/4$	teaspoon salt
1	teaspoon white wine vinegar
3–4	tablespoons slivered almonds, to top
	Confectioners' (icing) sugar, to dust
	Fresh raspberries or blueberries, to serve
1	cup (250 ml) plain fresh Greek yogurt, to serve

Serves 8 • Preparation 20 minutes + 15 minutes to cool • Cooking 30–40 minutes • Difficulty 1

1. Preheat the oven to 350°F (180°C/gas 4). Lightly grease a 9-inch (23-cm) springform pan and line the base with parchment paper.

2. Beat the egg yolks, lemon zest, and $1/4$ cup (50 g) of sugar in a bowl until pale and creamy.

3. Combine the almond meal, cinnamon, cardamom, and baking powder in a separate bowl. Add the almond mixture to the egg yolk mixture and beat with a wooden spoon until smooth.

4. Beat the egg whites in a bowl with an electric mixer on low speed. When bubbles start to form, add the salt and vinegar, and beat on medium. As the egg whites increase in volume, gradually add the remaining $1/4$ cup of sugar. Beat until soft peaks form.

5. Fold the egg whites into the almond mixture one large spoonful at a time.

6. Spoon the batter into the prepared pan. Sprinkle evenly with the slivered almonds. Bake for 30–40 minutes, until golden and firm to the touch.

7. Let cool on a wire rack for 15 minutes. Run a sharp knife around the edges of the pan. Release the pan sides, and carefully transfer to a serving plate or platter.

8. Dust with the confectioners' sugar, slice, and serve with a few raspberries and a dollop of yogurt.

starters & snacks

SEEDY CRACKERS with hummus

Crackers

1/4	cup (40 g) flax seeds
1/4	cup (40 g) chia seeds
1/2	cup (75 g) sunflower seeds
1/2	cup (75 g) pumpkin seeds
1/2	cup (80 g) sesame seeds
1/2	teaspoon sea salt flakes
1	teaspoon minced fresh rosemary
1	clove garlic, minced
1	cup (250 ml) water

Hummus

1	(14-ounce/400-g) can garbanzo beans (chickpeas), drained, with 3 tablespoons of the liquid reserved
2	cloves garlic, chopped
3	tablespoons freshly squeezed lemon juice
1/4	cup (60 ml) tahini
	Pinch of sweet ground paprika, to serve
	Carrot and celery sticks, to serve
	Fresh green beans, trimmed, to serve

Serves 4-6 • Preparation 15 minutes + 10 minutes to soften • Cooking 45-50 minutes • Difficulty 1

Crackers

1. Preheat the oven to 350°F (180°C/gas 4). Line a large baking sheet with parchment paper.

2. Mix all the seeds, salt, rosemary, and garlic in a bowl. Add the water gradually, stirring until well combined. Let sit for 10 minutes to soften the flax and chia seeds. Spread the batter out on the baking sheet to 1/4 inch (5 mm) thick.

3. Bake for 30 minutes. Remove from the oven and slice into crackers using a pizza wheel. Turn the crackers and replace on the baking sheet. Bake for 15-20 more minutes, until golden. Let cool completely on a wire rack.

Hummus

1. Chop the garbanzo beans, reserved liquid, garlic, lemon juice, and tahini in a food processor until smooth. Transfer to a serving bowl and dust with paprika.

2. Serve the crackers with the hummus and vegetables.

If you liked this recipe, you will love these as well.

ROSEMARY crackers

CHEESE straws

GLUTEN-FREE bread

GREEN PEA hummus

2   cups fresh shelled green peas
      (from 2 pounds/1 kg peas in
      pod)
1   (14-ounce/400-g) can
      garbanzo beans (chickpeas),
      drained and rinsed
$\frac{1}{2}$ cup chopped fresh parsley
1   clove garlic
$\frac{1}{3}$ cup (90 ml) plain, Greek-style
      yogurt
4   scallions (spring onions),
      trimmed and chopped
3   tablespoons freshly squeezed
      lemon juice
1   teaspoon ground cumin
2   tablespoons extra-virgin olive
      oil
1   teaspoon sea salt flakes
      Carrot and celery sticks,
      to serve

Serves 4–6 • Preparation 15 minutes • Difficulty 1

1. Combine the green peas, garbanzo beans, parsley, garlic, yogurt, scallions, lemon juice, cumin, oil, and salt in a food processor and chop until almost smooth. Leave a little bit of texture in the mixture.

2. Transfer to a serving dish, and serve with the crackers or vegetables.

TARAMASALATA

2   medium white potatoes, peeled and boiled

5   ounces (150 g) cod roe

1   small white onion, chopped

$^2/_3$ cup (150 ml) extra-virgin olive oil + extra, as required

Freshly squeezed juice of 1 lemon

Freshly ground sea salt and black pepper

Finely chopped parsley, to garnish

Gluten-free corn chips or rosemary crackers (see page 28)

Serves 6–8 • Preparation 15 minutes + 2 hours to chill • Cooking 20–25 minutes • Difficulty 2

1. Place the potatoes in a small pan of boiling water and simmer until tender, 20–25 minutes.

2. Combine the potatoes, cod roe, onion, oil, and lemon juice in the bowl of a food processor and chop until smooth. Add more oil if the mixture is too thick. Season with salt and pepper.

3. Transfer to a serving bowl, cover with plastic wrap (cling film), and refrigerate for at least 2 hours before serving.

4. Garnish with the parsley and serve with the corn chips or rosemary crackers.

These delicious crackers make a wonderful gluten-free alternative to wheat flour bread or crackers when serving with salads and soups. You can store them in an airtight container for 2–3 days.

ROSEMARY *crackers*

1³/₄ cups (175 g) almond meal
¹/₂ teaspoon sea salt flakes
2 tablespoons finely chopped fresh rosemary
1 tablespoon extra-virgin olive oil
1 large egg

Serves 6–8 • Preparation 15 minutes • Cooking 12–15 minutes
Difficulty 2

1. Preheat the oven to 350°F (180°C/gas 4).

2. Combine the almond meal, salt, and rosemary in a bowl. Whisk the oil and egg in another bowl. Stir the oil mixture into the almond mixture until well combined.

3. Roll the dough into a ball and roll between 2 sheets of parchment paper to ¹/₄ inch (5 mm) thick. Remove the top piece of parchment paper.

4. Transfer the bottom piece of parchment with the rolled out dough onto a large baking sheet. Cut the dough into 2-inch (5-cm) squares using a knife or pizza cutter.

5. Bake for 12-15 minutes, until pale golden brown.

6. Let the crackers cool on the baking sheet for at least 30 minutes before serving.

If you liked this recipe, you will love these as well.

SEEDY CRACKERS
with hummus

GLUTEN-FREE bread

SUN-DRIED TOMATO
loaf

TAPENADE

Serves 4-6 • Preparation 15 minutes • Difficulty 1

1¹/₂	cups (225 g) pitted black olives	1	tablespoon freshly squeezed lemon juice
¹/₂	cup fresh parsley leaves	3	tablespoons extra-virgin olive oil
2	cloves garlic, coarsely chopped		Freshly ground black pepper
1	tablespoon salt-cured capers, rinsed		Seedy crackers (see page 27), to serve (optional)
3	anchovy fillets, coarsely chopped		

1. Combine the olives, parsley, garlic, capers, and anchovies in a food processor and pulse until coarsely blended.

2. Add the lemon juice and gradually pour in the oil, blending to make a smooth paste. Season with pepper.

3. Serve immediately or store in an airtight container in the refrigerator for up to one week.

GUACAMOLE

Serves 4-6 • Preparation 10 minutes • Difficulty 1

2	avocados, halved lengthwise and pit removed		chopped
			Freshly ground sea salt and black pepper
2	tablespoons freshly squeezed lime juice		Dash of Tabasco sauce
1	clove garlic, minced	1	small tomato, chopped, to garnish
2	scallions (spring onions) thinly sliced		Gluten-free tortilla chips or seedy crackers (see page 27)
¹/₂	green birds' eye chili, seeded and finely		

1. Use a teaspoon to remove the flesh from one avocado and place in a food processor with the lime juice and garlic. Blend until smooth. Transfer to a medium bowl.

2. Peel and dice the remaining avocado and add to the puréed mixture. Add the scallions and chile and stir to combine. Season with salt, pepper, and Tabasco sauce. Garnish with the tomato.

3. Serve immediately or on the day of making.

PEAR, BRIE & WALNUT salad

Serves 4 • Preparation 10 minutes • Difficulty 1

¹/₄	cup (60 ml) extra-virgin olive oil	3	large ripe pears, cored and sliced
2	tablespoons balsamic vinegar	20	walnuts, coarsely chopped
	Sea salt flakes		Gluten-free bread (see page 38), to serve
3	cups (150 g) arugula (rocket) leaves		
8	ounces (250 g) Brie, sliced		

1. Whisk the oil, vinegar, and a pinch of salt with a fork in a small bowl to make a smooth dressing.

2. Arrange the arugula in a large shallow salad bowl. Arrange the Brie on the arugula. Top with the slices of pear.

3. Drizzle with the dressing. Sprinkle with the walnuts, and serve at once with the bread.

CHEESE & RADICCHIO salad

Serves 4-6 • Preparation 15 minutes • Cooking 5 minutes Difficulty 2

Vinaigrette

2	tablespoons white wine vinegar		
¹/₂	teaspoon sea salt		
	Pinch of sugar		
	Freshly ground black pepper		
5	tablespoons (75 ml) extra-virgin olive oil		
1	shallot, thinly sliced		

Salad

2	tablespoons honey
4	soft goat cheese rounds, about 1¹/₂ ounces (40 g) each
3	sprigs fresh thyme, coarsely chopped
2	heads red radicchio
6	cherry tomatoes, halved
	Rosemary crackers (see page 28), to serve

Vinaigrette

1. Whisk the vinegar, salt, sugar, and a good grinding of pepper in a small bowl. Whisk in the oil until blended. Stir the shallot into the vinaigrette and adjust the seasoning.

Salad

1 Drizzle the honey over the cheese and sprinkle with thyme. Place under a hot broiler (grill) for a few minutes, until the tops turn light golden.

2. Transfer the warm cheese to serving plates with the radicchio and tomatoes. Drizzle with the vinaigrette and serve warm with the crackers.

AVOCADO & BLUE CHEESE salads

Salad

1	cup (120 g) walnut halves
4	cups (200 g) arugula (rocket)
2	avocados, peeled, pitted and thinly sliced
2	cups (100 g) seedless red grapes, halved
1	mango, peeled, pitted and cut into small cubes
4	scallions (spring onions), thinly sliced
1/2	cup chopped fresh cilantro (coriander)
7	ounces (200 g) blue cheese, such as Roquefort, Gorgonzola piccante, or Danish, crumbled

Dressing

1/2	cup (120 ml) extra-virgin olive oil
2	teaspoons Dijon mustard
1/4	cup (60 ml) balsamic vinegar
	Freshly ground sea salt and black pepper

To Serve

Gluten-free bread (see page 38) or Seedy crackers (see page 25)

Serves 6–8 • Preparation 20 minutes • Difficulty 1

Salad

1. Dry-fry the walnuts in a small pan over medium heat, shaking often, until fragrant and crisp, 3–4 minutes.

2. Combine the arugula, avocados, grapes, mango, scallions, cilantro, cheese, and walnuts in a bowl. Toss well to combine. Transfer the salad into six to eight medium serving glasses.

Dressing

1. Whisk the oil, mustard, vinegar, salt, and pepper in a small bowl until emulsified.

2. Drizzle the dressing over the salads just before serving. Serve with the gluten-free bread or rosemary crackers.

If you liked this recipe, you will love these as well.

PEAR, BRIE & WALNUT salad

CHEESE & RADICCHIO salad

GRILLED POLENTA with green salsa

FRIED POLENTA with mushroom topping

Polenta

2	quarts (2 liters) cold water
1½	tablespoons coarse sea salt
3½	cups (500 g) quick-cooking polenta

Mushroom Sauce

2	tablespoons extra-virgin olive oil
2	cloves garlic, minced
2	pounds (1 kg) white mushrooms, stalks and caps coarsely chopped
2	tablespoons finely chopped fresh thyme + extra, to garnish
	Freshly ground sea salt and black pepper
2	cups (500 ml) vegetable oil, for frying

Serves 8 • Preparation 30 minutes + 2–12 hours to chill • Cooking 30–40 minutes • Difficulty 2

Polenta

1. Bring the water and salt to a boil in a large saucepan. Pour in the polenta, stirring all the time with a wooden spoon. Lower the heat and simmer, stirring often, for 10–12 minutes.

2. Line a large baking sheet with parchment paper. Spoon the polenta onto the baking sheet. Spread into a rectangle about ³⁄₄ inch (1.5 cm) thick. Cover with parchment and a another baking sheet. Top with cans or jars to press down on the polenta. Chill for at least 2 hours, or overnight.

Mushroom Sauce

1. Heat the olive oil in a pan over medium heat. Add the garlic and sauté until softened, 3–4 minutes. Add the mushrooms, thyme, salt, and pepper. Simmer until tender.

2. Cut the polenta into sixteen squares.

3. Heat the frying oil in a deep-fryer to 365°F (190°C). .

4. Fry the polenta in batches until golden, about 5 minutes each batch. Scoop out with a slotted spoon and drain on paper towels. Spoon the mushroom sauce onto the hot polenta. Garnish with the thyme, and serve immediately.

GRILLED POLENTA with green salsa

Polenta

6   cups (1.5 liters) water

1   teaspoon sea salt flakes

12   ounces (350 g) quick-cooking polenta

1   (14-ounce/400-g) can corn (sweetcorn), drained

1   red chili, seeded and finely chopped

¹/₂   cup (60 g) freshly grated Parmesan cheese

Green Salsa

2   avocados, peeled, pitted and cut into chunks

1   small cucumber, sliced very thinly lengthwise

4   scallions (spring onions), sliced

       Small bunch coarsely chopped fresh cilantro (coriander)

       Freshly squeezed juice of 2 limes

4   tablespoons (60 ml) extra-virgin olive oil

       Freshly ground sea salt and black pepper

Serves 6 • Preparation 15 minutes + 2–12 hours to chill • Cooking 25–35 minutes • Difficulty 2

Polenta

1. Bring the water and salt to a boil in a large saucepan. Pour in the polenta, stirring all the time with a wooden spoon. Lower the heat and simmer, stirring often, for 10–12 minutes.

2. Line a large baking sheet with parchment paper.

3. Stir the corn, chili, and cheese into the polenta, then spoon onto the baking sheet. Spread into a round about ³/₄ inch (1.5 cm) thick. Cover with parchment and a another baking sheet. Top with cans or jars to press down on the polenta. Chill for at least 2 hours, or overnight.

Green Salsa

1. Mix the avocados, cucumber, scallions, cilantro, lime juice, and 2 tablespoons of oil in a bowl. Season with salt and pepper.

2. Preheat a grill pan (griddle) over medium-high heat. Cut the polenta into 12 wedges. Brush both sides of each wedge with the remaining oil. Grill for 5 minutes on each side until marked with brown lines and heated through.

3. Serve warm, with the salsa.

Serve these crisp, cheesy straws with predinner drinks along with little bowls of olives, grapes, and artichoke hearts. They are also very good with soups and salads.

CHEESE straws

1¼	cups (125 g) almond flour
2	tablespoons coconut flour
2	tablespoons cornstarch (cornflour)
1	teaspoon xanthan gum
1	clove garlic, minced
¼	teaspoon sea salt flakes
5	tablespoons (75 g) butter, chilled and cut into small pieces
2-4	tablespoons iced water
1	cup (120 g) freshly grated sharp Cheddar cheese

Serves 4-6 • Preparation 15 minutes + 30 minutes to chill • Cooking 25–30 minutes • Difficulty 1

1. Combine the almond flour, coconut flour, cornstarch, xanthan gum, garlic, and salt in a food processor. Pulse a few times to combine. Add the butter and pulse until the mixture resembles fine crumbs.

2. With the processor on low speed, add the water 1 tablespoon at a time until the dough clumps together.

3. Remove from the food processor and shape into a flat disk. Cover with plastic wrap (cling film). Chill for 30 minutes.

4. Preheat the oven to 300°F (150 °C/gas 3) Line a large baking sheet with parchment paper.

5. Break off about 1 tablespoon of dough and roll it between your palms into a cigar shape. Continue to roll gently on a piece of parchment into a long thin stick.

6. Sprinkle with a few teaspoons of Cheddar, gently pressing the cheese into the stick to adhere. Transfer to the prepared baking sheet.

7. Bake for 25–30 minutes, until firm and golden brown. Remove from oven and let cool completely on the baking sheet before serving.

GLUTEN-FREE bread

2	cups (300 g) tapioca flour
3/4	cup (125 g) sorghum flour
1/2	cup (75 g) quinoa flour
2	tablespoons chia seeds, finely ground
2	tablespoons psyllium husks
2	teaspoons sea salt flakes
1/4	ounce (7 g/1 sachet) instant or active dry yeast or 1/2 ounce (15 g) fresh yeast
1 1/2	cups (375 ml) lukewarm water
2	large eggs, lightly beaten
2	tablespoons light olive oil
2	teaspoons honey
1/4	teaspoon apple cider vinegar
	Quinoa flakes, to sprinkle

Serves 6–8 • Preparation 20 minutes + 1 hour to prove • Cooking 40–50 minutes • Difficulty 2

1. Lightly butter an 8 1/2 x 4 1/2 inch (21 x 12-cm) loaf pan.

2. Combine the tapioca, sorghum, and quinoa flours with the ground chia, psyllium, and salt in a stand mixer fitted with a paddle attachment. If using instant yeast, sprinkle it into the bowl and mix on low speed to combine. If using active dry or fresh yeast, blend with a little of the water in a small bowl. Add the water, yeast mixture, eggs, oil, honey, and vinegar to the bowl with the flour and mix on low speed until a thick sticky batter forms, 3–4 minutes. It should resemble a thick muffin batter.

3. Spoon the batter into the prepared pan, spreading it evenly. Sprinkle with quinoa flakes. Cover with a clean cloth and set aside in a warm, draft free place to prove until increased in size by two-thirds, about 1 hour. .

4. Preheat the oven to 400°F (200°C/gas 6).

5. Bake for 40–50 minutes, until golden brown and the loaf sounds hollow when tapped on the base. Leave on the sheet to cool slightly. Place on a rack to cool completely.

SUN-DRIED TOMATO loaf

1¹/₃ cups (200 g) gluten-free white flour mix

1 teaspoon sea salt flakes

3 teaspoons gluten-free baking powder

1 cup (250 ml) buttermilk (or same amount of whole milk with a squeeze of lemon juice)

3 large eggs

1 teaspoon tomato purée

2 tablespoons extra-virgin olive oil

6–8 sundried tomatoes in oil, coarsely chopped

¹/₄ cup (30 g) freshly grated Parmesan cheese

Serves 6–8 • Preparation 20 minutes • Cooking 40–50 minutes
Difficulty 1

1. Preheat the oven to 350°F (180°C/gas 4).

2. Combine the flour mix, salt, and baking powder in a large bowl. Whisk the buttermilk, eggs, tomato purée, and oil in a separate bowl. Stir the buttermilk mixture into the dry, then add the sundried tomatoes and half the Parmesan.

3. Grease a 2-pound (1-kg) loaf pan and pour in the mixture. Sprinkle with the remaining Parmesan.

4. Bake for 40–50 minutes, until risen and golden brown. Cool in the pan for 15 minutes. Turn out onto a wire rack and let cool completely before serving.

Fragrant, cheesy pizza is one of the things that gluten-intolerant people most often miss. Follow this recipe to discover a wonderfully crisp crust and delicious topping.

Pizza needs a very hot oven to cook properly and we suggest you cook this one at 500°F (250°C/gas 10). Many older domestic ovens do not reach this temperature; if yours doesn't just bake at the highest possible temperature.

GLUTEN-FREE pizza

Tomato Sauce

1	tablespoon extra-virgin olive oil
2	cloves garlic, finely chopped
2	cups (500 ml) tomato passata
2	teaspoons tomato paste (concentrate)
1	teaspoon dried oregano
	Freshly ground sea salt and black pepper

Crust

$3/4$	cup (120 g) tapioca flour
$1/2$	cup (80 g) white rice flour
$1/3$	cup (40 g) garbanzo (chickpea) flour
$1/3$	cup (50 g) sorghum flour
2	teaspoons sugar
1	teaspoon xanthan gum
1	teaspoon sea salt flakes
1	($1/4$-ounce/7-g) package instant yeast
$1/2$	cup (120 ml) warm milk
$1/4$	cup (60 ml) warm water
2	large egg whites, lightly beaten
3	tablespoons + 1 teaspoon extra-virgin olive oil

Topping

4	teaspoons extra-virgin olive oil
8	ounces (250 g) fresh mozzarella, coarsely grated
2	tablespoons freshly grated Parmesan cheese
	Fresh basil leaves, to garnish
$1/2$	cup (120 g) light cream cheese (optional)

Serves 2–4 • Preparation 30 minutes + 30 minutes to prove • Cooking 15–20 minutes • Difficulty 2

Tomato Sauce

1. Heat the oil in a saucepan over medium heat. Add the garlic and sauté until softened, 2–3 minutes. Stir in the tomato passata, tomato paste, and oregano and simmer until thickened, 5–10 minutes. Season with salt and pepper.

Crust

1. Whisk the tapioca, rice, garbanzo, and sorghum flours, sugar, xanthan gum, salt, and yeast in a stand mixer fitted with a dough hook. Add the milk, water, egg whites, and 2 tablespoons of oil and beat on medium speed until the dough is very smooth and thick, about 5 minutes.

2. Preheat the oven to 500°F (250°C/gas 10). Place a pizza stone or large baking sheet in the oven to preheat.

3. Prepare two 12-inch (30-cm) squares of parchment paper. Divide the dough in half, shape each piece into a ball, and place on the paper. Coat each ball with 2 teaspoons of oil, then stretch into rounds about $1/4$ inch (5 mm) thick. Cover with a cloth and prove in a warm place for 30 minutes.

4. Slip one crust onto the pizza stone and bake for 5–10 minutes, until puffed, firm, and crisp. Transfer to a rack to cool. Bake the second crust in the same way.

Topping

1. Preheat the overhead broiler (grill) in the oven to medium-high. Transfer the crusts to baking sheets. Top with tomato sauce, mozzarella, and Parmesan. Drizzle with the oil.

2. Broil until the cheese is bubbling and brown, 5–8 minutes. Top with the cream cheese, if using, and basil, and serve hot.

CHICKEN SKEWERS with pesto

Pesto

$1/4$	cup (30 g) pine nuts, lightly toasted
1	clove garlic, chopped
$1/3$	cup (45 g) freshly grated Parmesan cheese
$1/2$	cup (120 ml) extra-virgin olive oil
3	cups (150 g) basil leaves
	Freshly ground sea salt and black pepper

Skewers

2	boneless, skinless chicken breast, cut into 24 long strips
24	wooden skewers
$1/3$	cup (50 g) chopped almond slivers
	Olive oil, for cooking
	Freshly ground sea salt and black pepper

Serves 4–6 • Preparation 30 minutes • Cooking 8–10 minutes
Difficulty 1

Pesto

1. Combine the pine nuts and garlic in a food processor and blend to make a coarse paste.

2. Add the cheese and half the oil and blend to combine. Add the basil and pulse until blended. Gradually add the remaining oil and blend until smooth. Season with salt and pepper.

Skewers

1. Preheat the overhead broiler (grill) in the oven to medium.

2. Combine the chicken with half the pesto in a bowl. Season with salt and pepper. Thread the chicken onto the skewers.

3. Lightly oil a baking dish and arrange the skewers in it in a single layer. Broil, turning often, for 8–10 minutes, until the chicken is cooked through and lightly browned.

4. Place in a serving dish and drizzle with the remaining pesto. Sprinkle with the almonds, and serve hot.

PORK MEATBALLS with sweet chili sauce

1   pound (500 g) ground (minced) pork
2   tablespoons soy sauce
1   tablespoon oyster sauce
4   cloves garlic, minced
2   teaspoons peeled and minced ginger
1   teaspoon ground cumin
1/2 teaspoon ground turmeric
1   small bunch cilantro (coriander), minced
1   scallion (spring onion), finely chopped
1   clove garlic, minced
1   teaspoon sea salt flakes
1   teaspoon freshly ground black pepper
3   tablespoons extra-virgin olive oil
    Sweet chili sauce, to dip

Serves 6–8 • Preparation 20 minutes • Cooking 10 minutes • Difficulty 1

1. Combine the pork, soy sauce, oyster sauce, garlic, ginger, cumin, turmeric, cilantro, scallion, salt, and pepper in a large bowl, mixing with your hands until well combined. Shape into sixteen even meatballs.

2. Heat the oil in a large frying pan over medium-high heat. Add the meatballs and cook, turning often, until cooked through and browned all over, about 10 minutes.

3. Transfer to a plate lined with paper towels to drain. Insert a toothpick into each one.

4. Serve hot, with a bowl of sweet chili sauce for dipping.

RED LENTIL SOUP with lime

Serves 6-8 • Preparation 20 minutes • Cooking 35-40 minutes • Difficulty 1

3	tablespoons sunflower oil	1½	cups (350 g) red lentils
1	large onion, finely chopped	8	cups (2 liters) chicken stock
1	stalk celery, finely chopped		Finely grated zest of ½ lime
1	carrot, finely chopped	1	bay leaf
1	clove garlic, minced	2	tablespoons fresh lime juice
½	teaspoon dried marjoram		Salt and freshly ground black pepper
½	teaspoon dried thyme	2	tablespoons finely chopped fresh parsley
1	teaspoon ground cumin		

1. Heat the oil in a pot over medium heat. Add the onion, celery, and carrot and sauté for 7-10 minutes.

2. Stir in the garlic, marjoram, lemon thyme, cumin, lentils, chicken stock, lime zest, and bay leaf, and bring to a boil. Cover and simmer until the lentils are soft, 20-25 minutes.

3. Discard the bay leaf. Purée with a handheld blender. Return to the heat. Season with salt and pepper and add lime juice to taste. Garnish with the parsley and serve hot.

LAMB & VEGETABLE soup

Serves 8 • Preparation 30 minutes + 12 hours to chill Cooking about 5 hours • Difficulty 2

1	shoulder lamb 3-4 pounds (1.5-2 kg), bone in	1	small rutabaga (swede), peeled and diced
2	teaspoons sea salt	1	small turnip, peeled and diced
2	teaspoons black peppercorns	1	small cabbage, sliced
1	large onion, sliced	3	stalks celery, sliced
3	large leeks, sliced	4	tablespoons finely chopped fresh parsley
3	medium carrots, sliced	6	medium potatoes, peeled and diced
1	parsnip, peeled and diced		

1. Put the lamb in a large soup pot. Cover with water and add the salt and peppercorns. Simmer until the meat falls off the bone, about 2 hours.

2. Remove the lamb and strain the stock left in the pot. Pull all the lamb from the bone, discarding the bone. Cut or break the meat into bite-size pieces.

3. Return the lamb and stock to the pot. Add the onion, leeks, carrots, parsnip, rutabaga, turnip, cabbage, celery, and 2 tablespoons of parsley. Cover and simmer over low heat for 2 hours, adding more water as required. Add the potatoes and simmer for 45 minutes. Let cool, then chill overnight.

4. Next day, reheat the soup over low heat for 30 minutes. Stir in the remaining parsley. Serve hot.

MEXICAN BEAN soup

Serves 8-10 • Preparation 30 minutes + 12 hours to soak Cooking about 1½ hours • Difficulty 1

1	pound (500 g) dried pinto beans	2	(14-ounce/400-g) cans tomatoes, with juice
3	tablespoons extra-virgin olive oil	1	tablespoon cumin seeds
2	onions, chopped	1	tablespoon oregano
2	large carrots, chopped		Freshly ground sea salt and black pepper
2	stalks celery, chopped	¼	cup (60 ml) dry sherry
3	cloves garlic, minced	2	tablespoons lime juice
	Bouquet garni of parsley, thyme, bay leaves and rosemary	1	avocado, diced
4	ounces (120 g) bacon, diced	2	scallions (spring onions), thinly sliced
		2	red chilies, minced

1. Soak the beans overnight in cold water. Heat the oil in a soup pot over low heat. Add the onions, carrots, celery, garlic, bouquet garni, and bacon. Cover and sweat until the vegetables are tender, 10-15 minutes.

2. Add the beans and water to cover. Bring to a boil then cover and simmer until tender, about 1 hour. Add the tomatoes, cumin, oregano, salt, pepper, sherry, and lime juice and simmer for 10 minutes.

3. Top with the avocado, scallions, chilies, and serve hot

LEEK & POTATO soup

Serves 6-8 • Preparation 15 minutes • Cooking 30-35 minutes • Difficulty 1

¼	cup (60 ml) extra-virgin olive oil	1	small bunch parsley, finely chopped + extra, to garnish
6	leeks, thinly sliced	6	medium-large potatoes, peeled and diced
1	large onion, finely chopped	4	cups (1 liter) vegetable stock
1	clove garlic, finely chopped		Freshly ground sea salt and black pepper
1	carrot, finely chopped		
1	stalk celery, finely chopped		

1. Heat the oil in a soup pot over medium-low heat. Add the leeks, onion, garlic, carrot, celery, and parsley and sauté until the vegetables are almost tender, about 10 minutes.

2. Add the potatoes and pour in the vegetable stock. Season with salt and pepper. Bring to a boil, then simmer over low heat until the potatoes are tender, 15-20 minutes.

3. Purée with a handheld blender until smooth. Return the pan to the heat for 2-3 minutes. Serve hot, garnished with a little extra parsley.

SUN-DRIED TOMATO & RICE *fritters*

3 tablespoons butter
1 tablespoon extra-virgin olive oil
1 onion, finely chopped
1 clove garlic, finely chopped
1 cup (200 g) Arborio rice
1/2 cup (75 g) sun-dried tomatoes, finely chopped
2 tablespoons finely chopped fresh oregano
1/2 cup (120 ml) dry white wine
3 1/2 cups (875 ml) vegetable stock, boiling
1/3 cup (50 g) freshly grated Parmesan cheese
Freshly ground sea salt and black pepper
3 1/2 ounces (100 g) mozzarella cheese, cut into small cubes
1 cup (150 g) cornmeal
4 cups (1 liter) vegetable oil, for deep frying

Serves 6–8 • Preparation 45 minutes + 1 1/2 hours to rest and chill
Cooking 25–35 minutes • Difficulty 3

1. Heat 2 tablespoons of butter with the oil in a large saucepan over medium heat. Add the onion and garlic and sauté until softened, 3–4 minutes. Add the rice, tomatoes, and oregano and cook, stirring constantly, for 2–3 minutes.

2. Pour in the wine and stir until evaporated. Decrease the heat to medium-low and begin adding the stock, one ladleful at a time. Cook and stir until each addition has been absorbed and the rice is tender, 15–18 minutes. Stir in the Parmesan and remaining 1 tablespoon of butter. Season with salt and pepper.

3. Line a baking sheet with parchment paper. Spread the risotto on top and set aside to cool, about 1 hour.

4. Roll the rice into walnut-size balls. Push a piece of cheese into the center of each one. Roll in the cornmeal to coat. Chill until firm, about 30 minutes.

5. Heat the frying oil in a deep-fryer to 365°F (190°C).

6. Fry in batches until golden, about 5 minutes. Scoop out with a slotted spoon and drain on paper towels. Serve hot .

QUINOA fritters

1 cup (200 g) quinoa
2 cups (500 ml) vegetable stock
1 bay leaf
2 tablespoons extra-virgin olive oil
1 large onion, finely chopped
2 cloves garlic, finely chopped
1 tablespoon chili paste
1/2 cup (60 g) freshly grated Parmesan cheese
2 tablespoons finely chopped fresh parsley
2 cups (300 g) cornmeal
1/4 cup (60 g) cream cheese, softened
4 large eggs, lightly beaten
Freshly ground sea salt and black pepper
4 cups (1 liter) vegetable oil, for deep frying

Serves 4-6 • Preparation 20 minutes + 2-12 hours to chill • Cooking 30 minutes • Difficulty 2

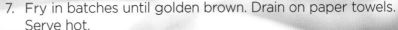

1. Combine the quinoa and vegetable stock in a pot. Add the bay leaf and bring to a boil. Cover and simmer over low heat until the liquid is absorbed, about 15 minutes. Turn off the heat and let rest for 10 minutes. Discard the bay leaf.

2. Heat the olive oil in a large frying pan over medium heat. Add the onion, garlic, and chili paste and sauté until softened, 3-4 minutes.

3. Stir the onion mixture into the quinoa, along with the cheese, parsley, 1/3 cup (50 g) of cornmeal, and cream cheese. Stir in two eggs. Season with salt and pepper. Chill the quinoa mixture for 2 hours, or overnight.

4. Break the two remaining eggs into a shallow bowl and whisk in a pinch of salt. Put the remaining cornmeal into another shallow bowl or dish.

5. Shape the quinoa mixture into croquettes. Dip into the egg mixture, then into the cornmeal to coat.

6. Heat the frying oil in a deep-fryer to 365°F (190°C). .

7. Fry in batches until golden brown. Drain on paper towels. Serve hot.

These attractive little pies will be a welcome addition to a gluten-free buffet spread. They also make a hearty snack or a tasty light lunch.

MINI CHILI BEEF pies

Pastry

1¼	cups (170 g) white or brown rice flour
½	cup (80) sweet rice flour
½	cup (80 g) tapioca starch
1	teaspoon xanthan gum
1	cup (250 g) chilled salted butter, cut into small pieces
4	tablespoons (60 ml) water + extra, as required

Chili Beef

1	tablespoon extra-virgin olive oil
1	small onion, chopped
2	teaspoons hot chili powder
1	teaspoon ground cumin
8	ounces (250 g) ground (minced) beef
⅓	cup (90 ml) tomato purée
⅔	cup (150 ml) beef stock
	Pinch of ground cinnamon
1	cup (200 g) canned white kidney beans, drained and rinsed
	Freshly ground sea salt and black pepper

Topping

12	ounces (350 g) potatoes, peeled and cut into chunks
¼	cup (60 ml) sour cream
2	tablespoons snipped fresh chives, to garnish

Serves 6–12 • Preparation 45 minutes + 1 hour to chill • Cooking 50–55 minutes • Difficulty 2

Pastry

1. Combine both rice flours, tapioca starch, and xanthan gum in a bowl. Rub or cut in the butter until the mixture resembles coarse crumbs. Stir in 4 tablespoons of water. If too dry, add more water, 1 tablespoon at a time.

2. Shape the dough into a ball, wrap in plastic wrap (cling film), and chill in the refrigerator for 1 hour.

Chili Beef

1. Heat the oil in a frying pan over medium heat and sauté the onion until softened, 3–4 minutes. Add the chili powder and cumin and sauté for 1 minute. Stir in the beef and cook for 5 minutes. Add the tomato purée, beef stock, and cinnamon. Bring to a boil, then simmer on low heat until reduced, 15–20 minutes. Add the beans 5 minutes before the end of cooking. Season with salt and pepper.

2. Preheat the oven to 400°F (200°C/gas 6).

3. Roll out the pastry on a lightly floured work surface until about ¼ inch (5 mm) thick. Using a 3-inch (7-cm) pastry cutter, stamp out 12 circles from the pastry. Use them to line a 12-hole standard muffin pan. Prick the bases with a fork, and bake for 10 minutes. Cool on a wire rack.

Topping

1. Cook the potatoes in boiling water until tender. Drain and mash with the sour cream. Season with salt and pepper.

2. Spoon the chili into the pastry cases and top with a spoonful of mash. Bake for 15 minutes, until golden. Serve hot, garnished with chives

main courses

GLUTEN-FREE QUICHE
with mushrooms & goat cheese

Serves 4–6 • Preparation 30 minutes + 10 minutes to cool • Cooking about 1 hour • Difficulty 2

Pastry

2	cups (200 g) finely ground almond meal
2	cloves garlic, minced
1	tablespoon finely chopped fresh thyme
1/2	teaspoon sea salt flakes
1/4	teaspoon freshly ground pepper
1/3	cup (90 ml) extra-virgin olive oil
1	tablespoon water + extra, as required

Filling

1	tablespoon extra-virgin olive oil
4	ounces (120 g) sliced white mushrooms
	Freshly ground sea salt and black pepper
3	cups (150 g) coarsely chopped arugula (rocket)
6	large eggs
1/3	cup (90 ml) milk
1/2	teaspoon sea salt flakes
1/4	teaspoon red pepper flakes
5	ounces (150 g) goat cheese, crumbled

Pastry

1. Preheat the oven to 400°F (200°C/gas 6). Lightly grease a 10-inch (25-cm) tart pan.

2. Combine the almond meal, garlic, thyme, salt, and pepper in a large bowl. Pour in the oil and water and stir until the mixture is thoroughly combined. Press the dough evenly into the bottom and about 1 1/4 inches (3 cm) up the sides of the prepared pan.

3. Bake for 18–20 minutes, until pale golden brown and firm to the touch. Leave the oven on.

Filling

1. Heat the oil in a large frying pan over medium heat. Add the mushrooms, season with salt and pepper and simmer, stirring often, until tender, about 5 minutes. Add the arugula and stir until wilted, about 30 seconds. Set aside.

2. Whisk the eggs, milk, salt, and red pepper flakes in a bowl. Stir in the goat cheese and the mushroom and arugula mixture.

3. Spoon the egg mixture into the pre-baked crust and return to the oven for 30 minutes, until the center is set and cooked through.

4. Let the quiche cool for 10 minutes in the pan, then slice and serve warm.

POLENTA with meat sauce

Meat Sauce

2	tablespoons extra-virgin olive oil
2	onions, finely chopped
2	carrots, finely chopped
2	stalks celery, finely chopped
2	cloves garlic, finely chopped
2	gluten-free Italian sausages, skins removed, crumbled
1	pound (500 g) ground (minced) beef
1	tablespoon cornstarch (cornflour)
1/2	cup (120 ml) red wine
1	pound (500 g) tomatoes, peeled and chopped
1	tablespoon finely chopped fresh parsley
1/4	teaspoon ground nutmeg
2	bay leaves
	Freshly ground sea salt and black pepper

Polenta

2	quarts (2 liters) cold water
1 1/2	teaspoons coarse sea salt
3 1/2	cups (500 g) quick-cooking polenta
1/2	cup (60 g) freshly grated Parmesan cheese

Serves 6–8 • Preparation 30 minutes + 5–10 minutes to stand • Cooking about 2 1/2–3 1/2 hours • Difficulty 1

Meat Sauce

1. Heat the oil in a medium saucepan over low heat. Add the onions, carrots, and celery. Cover and simmer for 25–30 minutes, stirring often. Add the garlic and sausage, turn the heat up to high, and add the beef. Cook until browned.

2. Stir in the flour. Pour in the wine and cook until it has evaporated. Add the tomatoes, parsley, nutmeg, bay leaf, salt, and pepper. Partially cover the pan and simmer for 2–3 hours over low heat, adding a little water as required to keep it moist.

Polenta

1. Bring the water and salt to a boil in a large saucepan. Pour in the polenta, stirring all the time with a wooden spoon. Lower the heat and simmer, stirring often, for 10–12 minutes.

2. Pour the polenta onto a large serving platter or individual serving dishes. Spoon with the meat sauce over the top, sprinkle with Parmesan, and serve hot.

BAKED POLENTA with ricotta & tomato sauce

6 cups (1.5 liters) water
1 teaspoon sea salt
12 ounces (350 g) quick-cooking polenta
8 ounces (250 g) fresh ricotta cheese, drained
3 tablespoons extra-virgin olive oil
3 tablespoons butter
1 onion, finely chopped
3 tablespoons finely chopped fresh parsley
2 (14-ounce/400 g) cans tomatoes, with juice
Freshly ground black pepper
1½ cups (180 g) freshly grated Parmesan cheese

Serves 4–6 • Preparation 30 minutes + 5–10 minutes to stand • Cooking 50–60 minutes • Difficulty 2

1. Bring the water and salt to a boil in a large saucepan. Pour in the polenta, stirring all the time with a wooden spoon. Lower the heat and simmer, stirring often, for 10–12 minutes.

2. Preheat the oven to 350°F (180°C/gas 4). Press the ricotta through a fine-mesh sieve.

3. Heat the oil and butter in a large frying pan over medium heat. Add the onion and sauté until softened, 3–4 minutes. Add the parsley and tomatoes. Mix well. Season with salt and pepper. Simmer over low heat for 15 minutes.

4. Drizzle a work surface with cold water and turn the hot polenta out onto it. Spread to ½ inch (1 cm) thick. Slice the polenta and arrange a layer in an oiled baking dish. Add half the ricotta and spoon one-third of the sauce over the top. Sprinkle with Parmesan. Add another layer of polenta, the remaining ricotta, and half of the remaining sauce. Sprinkle with Parmesan then cover with the remaining polenta. Top with the remaining sauce and sprinkle with the remaining Parmesan.

5. Bake until golden brown, 20–25 minutes. Let stand for 5–10 minutes before serving.

Vary the vegetables in this tasty stew according to the season and what you have in the refrigerator.

VEGETABLE STEW with soft polenta

Stew

2	tablespoons extra-virgin olive oil
5	cloves garlic, minced
2	large leeks, white and pale green parts sliced into thin rounds
2	carrots, diced
12	ounces (350 g) sliced cremini mushrooms
1	sweet potato, diced
2	zucchini (courgettes), diced
	Freshly ground sea salt and black pepper
2	(14-ounce/400-g) cans chopped tomatoes, with juice
	Freshly ground sea salt and black pepper
2	(14-ounce/400-g) cans white beans, rinsed and drained
¼	cup chopped fresh parsley + extra, to garnish
¼	cup fresh basil + extra, to garnish

Polenta

12	ounces (350 g) quick-cooking polenta
8	cups (2 liters) vegetable stock

Serves 4–6 • Preparation 15 minutes • Cooking 25–35 minutes Difficulty 1

Stew

1. Heat the oil in a large saucepan over medium heat. Add the garlic and leeks and sauté until softened, 3–4 minutes. Add the carrots, mushrooms, sweet potato, and zucchini and sauté for 4–5 minutes. Season with salt and pepper. Add the tomatoes and simmer on low heat for 15 minutes.

Polenta

1. Bring the stock to a boil in a large pot. Pour in the polenta, stirring all the time with a wooden spoon. Lower the heat and simmer, stirring often, for 10–12 minutes.

2. Stir the beans into the stew and simmer until heated through. Stir in the herbs and remove from the heat.

3. Spoon the soft polenta into four to six serving plates. Spoon the vegetable stew over the top, garnish with extra herbs, and serve hot.

If you liked this recipe, you will love these as well.

GRILLED POLENTA
with green salsa

POLENTA
with meat sauce

BAKED POLENTA
with ricotta & tomato sauce

SEAFOOD rice

1	pound (500 g) mussels, in shell
1	pound (500 g) clams, in shell
4	tablespoons (60 ml) extra-virgin olive oil
1	onion, finely chopped
2	cloves garlic, finely chopped
1	small red chili, seeded and finely chopped
14	ounces (400 g) squid, cleaned and cut into rings
6	large tomatoes, peeled and cut into cubes
	Freshly ground sea salt and black pepper
2	cups (400 g) Italian risotto rice (Arborio)
1/4	cup (60 ml) white wine
6	cups (1.5 liters) vegetable stock, boiling
1	pound (500 g) shrimp, shelled
2	tablespoons butter
2-3	tablespoons finely chopped fresh parsley, to garnish

Serves 4-6 • Preparation 20 minutes • Cooking 30-40 minutes
Difficulty 2

1. Put the mussels and clams in a large pot over medium-high heat with a little water, cover, and cook until they are all open, about 5 minutes. Discard any that do not open.

2. Heat 2 tablespoons of oil in a large saucepan over medium heat. Add the onion and sauté until softened, 3-4 minutes. Stir in the garlic and chili. Add the squid and cook for 5-7 minutes over medium heat. Add the tomatoes, season with salt and pepper, and continue cooking over low heat.

3. Heat the remaining oil in a medium frying pan, add the rice and stir over high heat for 2 minutes.

4. Add the rice to the squid mixture. Pour in the wine and cook until it has evaporated. Pour in enough stock to generously cover the rice. Lower the heat, cover, and cook until the rice is tender, about 15 minutes.

5. Add the shrimp, mussels, and clams and cook until heated through. Stir in the butter. Garnish with the parsley, and serve hot.

SHRIMP fried rice

1 tablespoon oyster sauce
1 tablespoon soy sauce
1 teaspoon sea salt flakes
  Freshly ground black pepper
1 teaspoon cornstarch (cornflour) mixed with 2 teaspoons water
4 cups (400 g) cooked jasmine or other long-grain rice
20 medium shrimp (prawn), shelled, deveined, and coarsely chopped
6 tablespoons (90 ml) peanut oil
2 large eggs, lightly beaten
1 onion, diced
4 ounces (120 g) ham, diced
½ cup (75 g) frozen peas
2 scallions (green onions), sliced

Serves 4–6 • Preparation 15 minutes + 15 minutes to marinate • Cooking 15 minutes • Difficulty 1

1. Combine the oyster sauce, soy sauce, salt, pepper, and cornstarch mixture in a bowl. Add the shrimp and toss gently to coat. Let marinate for 15 minutes, then drain.

2. Heat 1 tablespoon of oil in a wok over medium-high heat. Pour in half of the egg mixture and cook until firm, turning once. Slip out of the wok onto a cutting board. Roll loosely and slice into thin strips. Repeat with remaining egg.

3. Add 2 tablespoons of the remaining oil to the wok. Stir-fry the onion and shrimp until the onion is just softened and the shrimp are turning pink, 2–3 minutes. Set aside.

4. Add 2 tablespoons of oil to the wok. Stir-fry the ham and peas until tender, about 2 minutes. Remove and set aside.

5. Add the remaining 1 tablespoon of oil, decrease the heat to medium, and stir-fry the rice until heated through, 2–3 minutes. Add the shrimp, onion, peas, and ham, mixing well. Serve hot topped with the eggs and scallions.

HARISSA FISH with potatoes

Serves 6 • Preparation 20 minutes • Cooking 15–20 minutes
Difficulty 1

2	pounds (1 kg) new potatoes, halved		black pepper
4	cloves garlic, minced	2	tablespoons harissa paste
1	cup (250 ml) plain yogurt	3	tablespoons extra-virgin olive oil
1	tablespoon fresh cream	6	firm white fish fillets, such as cod, snapper, halibut, or whiting, skinned (about 5 ounces/150 g each)
1½	teaspoons ground coriander		
2	tablespoons chopped fresh mint + extra		
	Salt and freshly ground		

1. Boil the potatoes until tender, 10–15 minutes. Drain.

2. Combine the garlic, yogurt, cream, coriander, and chopped mint in a bowl. Toss with the warm potatoes. Season with salt and pepper. Set aside.

3. Thin the harissa paste with 1 tablespoon of oil and smear over the fish fillets.

4. Heat the remaining oil in a frying pan over medium-high heat. Fry the fish for 2–3 minutes each side.

5. Transfer the potato salad to serving plates and place the fish on top. Serve warm.

CHICKEN with corn salsa

Serves 4 • Preparation 15 minutes • Cooking 12–15 minutes
Difficulty 1

Chicken

2	teaspoons ras el hanout (Moroccan spice mix)	1	cucumber, diced
		1	small red onion, finely chopped
2	tablespoons extra-virgin olive oil	2	tablespoons freshly squeezed lemon juice
4	small boneless, skinless chicken breasts, halved	2	tablespoons finely chopped fresh cilantro (coriander)
Salsa			
2	cups (250 g) canned corn (sweet corn), drained	2	tablespoons extra-virgin olive oil
2	tomatoes, diced		Salt and freshly ground black pepper

Chicken

1. Mix the ras el hanout with the oil in a small bowl. Brush the chicken with the mixture.

2. Place a grill pan (griddle) over medium-high heat. Grill the chicken until cooked, 5–7 minutes each side.

Salsa

1. Mix the corn, tomatoes, cucumber, onion, lemon juice, cilantro, and oil in a small bowl. Season with salt and pepper.

2. Serve the chicken hot with the salsa.

SALT & PEPPER squid

Serves 4–6 • Preparation 15 minutes • Cooking 15–20 minutes • Difficulty 2

6	medium squid tubes	1	teaspoon coriander seeds
2	tablespoons freshly squeezed lemon juice	4	cups (1 liter) canoli oil
2	tablespoons peppercorns	¾	cup (125 g) rice flour
2	tablespoons sea salt	¼	cup (30 g) cornstarch (cornflour)

1. Score the squid on one side, making a crisscross pattern with a sharp knife. Cut into 2-inch (5-cm) pieces. Toss with the lemon. Chill for 30 minutes.

2. Dry-fry the peppercorns, salt, and coriander in a small frying pan over medium heat until fragrant, about 30 seconds. Pound or grind to a fine powder.

3. Pour the oil into a deep-fryer over medium heat and heat to 365°F (190°C).

4. Drain the squid and pat dry with paper towels. Sift both flours and the spice mix into a medium bowl. Add half of the squid and toss to coat.

5. Fry the squid in two batches until golden, 2–3 minutes each batch. Drain on paper towels. Serve hot.

CHICKEN & RICE Tokyo-style

Serves 4 • Preparation 15 minutes • Cooking 20–25 minutes
Difficulty 1

1¼	cups (250 g) long-grain rice	4	cloves garlic, finely chopped
¼	cup (60 ml) peanut oil	3	boneless, skinless chicken breasts
¼	cup (60 ml) light soy sauce	2	large eggs, beaten
¼	cup (60 ml) mirin	4	scallions (green onions), thinly sliced
2	teaspoons freshly grated ginger		

1. Cook the rice in salted over medium heat until tender, 12–15 minutes. Drain well and set aside.

2. Mix 2 tablespoons of peanut oil, the soy sauce, mirin, ginger, and half the garlic in a small dish. Add the chicken and coat well.

3. Heat a grill pan (griddle) over medium-high. Grill the chicken until cooked, 5–7 minutes on each side.

4. Meanwhile, heat 2 teaspoons of oil in a wok or large frying pan over medium heat. Add the eggs and stir-fry until scrambled, about 1 minute. Remove from the pan and set aside.

5. Sauté the scallions and remaining garlic in the remaining oil in the same pan for 2 minutes. Add the rice and return the eggs to the wok. Stir-fry for 1 minute. Serve hot with the chicken.

GRILLED WHITE FISH with fragrant rice

Snapper

4	red snapper fillets, skinned (about 5 ounces/150 g each)
1	large mild red chili, sliced
2	teaspoons sea salt flakes
1	tablespoon grated ginger
	Finely grated zest and juice of 1 unwaxed lemon
1/4	cup (60 ml) sake (rice wine)
2	tablespoons sesame oil
	Lemon wedges to serve

Rice

1 1/2	cups (250 g) jasmine rice
2	tablespoons peanut oil
1	stalk lemongrass, bruised
1/2	inch piece (1 cm) fresh ginger, peeled
1	medium carrot, cut into matchsticks
1	small green chili, thinly sliced
	Handful fresh basil leaves
1	teaspoon sesame oil
2-3	teaspoons sake (rice wine)
1	red chili, thinly sliced
1	tablespoon toasted sesame seeds

Serves 6 • Preparation 20 minutes + 30 minutes to marinate • Cooking 15–20 minutes • Difficulty 1

Snapper

1. Place the fillets on a board and make three deep slashes with a sharp knife into each one. Push a few slices of chili into each slash and place the fillets in a shallow dish.

2. Mix the salt, ginger, and lemon zest and juice in a small bowl. Spoon the mixture over the snapper fillets. Cover and let marinate in the refrigerator for at least 30 minutes.

Rice

1. Cook the rice in a medium pot of lightly salted boiling water until tender, 10–12 minutes. Drain well.

2. Heat the oil in a wok over medium heat. Add the lemongrass, ginger, carrot, and green chili. Stir-fry for 2 minutes. Add the rice and basil and stir-fry until hot, 2–3 minutes.

3. Remove the lemongrass and ginger. Sprinkle with the sesame oil, sake, red chili, and sesame seeds. Set aside.

4. Sprinkle the fish with the sake, rubbing it into the flesh.

5. Heat a grill pan (griddle) until very hot. Brush the fillets with oil and grill until cooked through, 2–3 minutes on each side. Serve hot with the rice and lemon wedges.

SALMON STEAKS with spicy pak choy & rice

4	salmon steaks (about 5 ounces/150 g) each
	Sea salt and freshly ground black pepper
1	pak choy
3	tablespoons peanut oil
1	large onion, thinly sliced
1½	inches (4 cm) fresh ginger, peeled and thinly sliced
3	large tomatoes, seeded and chopped
1	long red chili, seeded and thinly sliced
1	teaspoon sugar
¾	cup (200 ml) coconut milk
¾	cup (200 ml) water
	Soy sauce to taste
	Freshly squeezed juice of 1 lime
½	cup chopped fresh cilantro (coriander) leaves
	Steamed rice, to serve

Serves 4 • Preparation 20 minutes • Cooking 35–40 minutes
Difficulty 2

1. Season the salmon with salt and pepper and set aside. Cut the leaves from the pak choy stalks. Coarsely shred the leaves with a knife and cut the stalks into small pieces.

2. Heat the oil in a wok or deep frying pan over medium heat. Add the onion, ginger, and pak choy stalks, and sauté until the onion is pale gold, 5–6 minutes.

3. Add the tomatoes, chili, and sugar, and simmer for 5 minutes, stirring often. Pour in the coconut milk and water. Season with salt and pepper. Bring to a boil, stirring constantly, then simmer over low heat for 15 minutes.

4. Stir in the pak choy leaves, add 3–4 shakes of soy sauce, and sprinkle with the lime juice. Place the salmon steaks in one layer on top of the sauce, spooning some of it over the fish. Cover with a tight-fitting lid or aluminum foil. Simmer until the fish is cooked through, 8–10 minutes.

5. Transfer the steaks with the sauce onto a serving dish. Spoon the remaining sauce over the top and sprinkle with cilantro. Serve hot with rice.

This tasty pie is great on cold winter evenings and hearty enough to serve as a meal in itself.

CURRIED CHICKEN & VEGETABLE pie

Pastry

$1/2$	cup (80) brown rice flour
$1/2$	cup (80) millet flour
$1/2$	cup (80) sorghum flour
$1/2$	cup (80 g) oat flour
1	teaspoon xanthan gum
1	cup (250 g) chilled butter, cut into small pieces
4-8	tablespoons (60-120 ml) water

Filling

2	tablespoons extra-virgin olive oil
1	onion, finely chopped
2	cloves garlic, chopped
1	green chili, finely chopped
2	boneless, skinless chicken breast, cut into small cubes
1	tablespoon garam masala
1	teaspoon ground turmeric and ground cumin
2	carrots, cubed
1	parsnip, cubed
1	small head (250 g) cauliflower, in florets
1	zucchini (courgette), cubed
$1/2$	cup (75 g) frozen peas
1	cup (250 ml) water
2	tablespoons butter
2	tablespoons cornstarch (cornflour) or potato starch
4	tablespoons plain yogurt
3	tablespoons chopped fresh cilantro (coriander)
2	tablespoons milk

Serves 4-6 • Preparation 30 minutes + 1 hour to chill • Cooking 40-45 minutes • Difficulty 2

Pastry

1. Combine the rice flour, millet flour, sorghum flour, tapioca starch, and xanthan gum in a bowl. Cut in the butter until the mixture resemble coarse crumbs. Stir in 4 tablespoons of water. If too dry, add more water, 1 tablespoon at a time.

2. Shape the dough into a ball, wrap in plastic wrap (cling film), and chill in the refrigerator for 1 hour.

3. Preheat the oven to 400°F (200°C/gas 6).

Filling

1. Heat the oil in a large frying pan over medium heat. Add the onion, garlic, and chili and sauté until softened, 3-4 minutes. Stir in the chicken, garam masala, turmeric, and cumin and sauté until browned, 3-5 minutes.

2. Add the carrots, parsnip, cauliflower, zucchini, peas, and water to the pan and simmer for 5 minutes. Drain, reserving the cooking liquid.

3. Melt the butter in a small pan, stir in the cornstarch, and cook for 1 minute. Add the reserved cooking liquid and cook and stir until thickened. Remove from the heat and stir in the yogurt, cilantro, vegetables, and seasoning.

4. Spoon the mixture into a large pie dish. Brush the rim with water. Roll out the pastry and use to cover the pie. Trim the edges and press firmly to seal. Cut 2-3 slashes in the top for steam to escape. Brush with the milk.

5. Bake for 25-30 minutes, until puffed and golden. Serve hot.

TURKEY LOAF wrapped in cabbage

1½ pounds (750 g) ground (minced) turkey breast

5 ounces (150 g) gluten-free pork sausages, crumbled

½ cup (60 g) bacon, chopped

½ cup (60 g) freshly grated Parmesan cheese

1 large egg + 1 large yolk

½ cup (100 g) well-cooked rice

Dash of nutmeg

Freshly ground sea salt and black pepper

8–10 leaves Savoy cabbage

2 shallots, sliced

2 cups (500 g) tomatoes, peeled and chopped

⅓ cup (90 ml) extra-virgin olive oil

½ cup (120 ml) white wine

½ cup (120 ml) beef stock

Serves 4 • Preparation 45 minutes • Cooking 1½ hours • Difficulty 2

1. Preheat the oven to 400°F (200°C/gas 6). Combine the turkey, sausage, bacon, Parmesan, eggs, rice, nutmeg, salt, and pepper in a large bowl and mix well.

2. Parboil the cabbage leaves in salted water for 4–5 minutes. Drain well. Arrange the leaves on a work surface to form a rectangle; they should be overlapping. Place the turkey mixture in the middle and shape into a meat loaf. Wrap the leaves around the turkey, taking care not to tear them. Tie with kitchen string.

3. Transfer the turkey loaf to an ovenproof dish with the shallots, tomatoes, and oil. Bake for 1¼ hours, basting frequently with the wine. When all the wine has been added, continue basting with the stock.

4. Slice and serve hot with the sauces from the baking dish spooned over the top.

CHICKEN CASSEROLE
with gluten-free dumplings

Serves 8 • Preparation 30 minutes • Cooking 2 hours • Difficulty 2

Casserole

8	large chicken pieces
	Salt and freshly ground black pepper
3	tablespoons cornstarch (cornflour)
3	tablespoons extra-virgin olive oil
3	onions, peeled and cut into wedges
8	ounces (250 g) pancetta
3	cloves garlic, thinly sliced
12	ounces (350 g) large flat mushrooms, sliced
2	bay leaves
6	strips peeled unwaxed orange zest
1	cup (250 ml) red wine
1½	cups (370 ml) chicken stock

Dumplings

½	cup (75 g) gluten-free flour
1½	teaspoons baking soda (bicarbonate of soda)
	Freshly ground sea salt and black pepper
1	teaspoon dried oregano
⅔	cup (150 g) frozen butter
1½	teaspoons cider vinegar

Casserole

1. Preheat the oven to 325°F (170°C/gas 3). Season the chicken with salt and pepper. Dust with 2 tablespoons of cornflour. Heat the oil in a Dutch oven and brown the chicken on high heat, 5–10 minutes. Set the chicken aside.

2. Add the onions and pancetta and sauté over medium heat until browned, about 5 minutes. Add the garlic and remaining cornflour and cook and stir for 1 minute.

3. Add the mushrooms, bay leaves, orange zest, wine, and chicken stock. Return the chicken to the pan and bring to a boil. Cover and bake in the oven for 1 hour.

Dumplings

1. Combine the flour, baking soda, salt, pepper, and oregano in a bowl. Grate in the butter and rub in until it resembles coarse crumbs. Add the vinegar and a few drops of cold water and shape into a ball. Divide into eight even pieces and gently roll into round balls.

2. Remove the casserole from the oven after 1 hour and sit the dumplings on top. Cover and bake for 20 minutes, then flip the dumplings and cook for 20 more minutes. Serve hot.

Osso buco is a classic Milanese dish. Its name means "bone with a hole." The traditional recipe does not include tomatoes but we think it adds extra flavor. We have also included a chopped fresh parsley gremolada garnish.

OSSO BUCO with gremolada

Osso Buco

6	veal hind shanks, cut in 1$1/2$-inch (4-cm) thick slices
$1/2$	cup (75 g) cornstarch (cornflour)
	Freshly ground sea salt and black pepper
$1/4$	cup (60 ml) extra-virgin olive oil
3	tablespoons butter
1	carrot, finely chopped
1	onion, finely chopped
1	stalk celery, finely chopped
4	sage leaves, torn
1	cup (250 ml) dry white wine
1	cup (250 ml) beef stock + extra, as required
3	tablespoons tomatoes, peeled and diced

Gremolada

	Finely chopped zest of 1 unwaxed lemon
1	clove garlic, finely chopped
2	tablespoons finely chopped fresh parsley

Serves 6 • Preparation 25 minutes • Cooking 2 hours • Difficulty 2

Osso Buco

1. Make 4–5 incisions around the edge of each shank to stop them curling up during cooking. Dredge the shanks in the cornstarch and season with salt and pepper.

2. Heat the oil in a large, heavy-bottomed saucepan over medium-high heat and cook the shanks for 3–4 minutes on both sides. Remove and set aside.

3. Melt the butter in the pan and add the carrot, onion, celery, and sage. When the vegetables are soft, add the meat and cook for a few minutes. Pour in the wine and cook until evaporated. Add the beef stock and tomatoes, and season with salt and pepper.

4. Cover and simmer over low heat until the meat is very tender, about 1$1/2$ hours, adding extra stock as required to keep the sauce moist.

Gremolada

1. When the meat is cooked, stir in the lemon zest, garlic, and parsley.

2. Serve the meat hot with boiled or steamed rice or a classic Milanese risotto.

BEEF NOODLE stir-fry

2	pounds (1 kg) beef tenderloin, cut into thin strips
5	tablespoons (75 ml) dark soy sauce
5	tablespoons (75 ml) apple juice
1	teaspoon dried red pepper flakes
2	cloves garlic, finely chopped
1	medium papaya (pawpaw), peeled and cut into small cubes
10	cherry tomatoes, halved
12	ounces (350 g) rice stick noodles
3	tablespoons peanut oil
2	stalks celery, sliced
2	tablespoons finely chopped fresh ginger
5	cups (250 g) baby spinach leaves

Serves 4–6 • Preparation 15 minutes + 2 hours to marinate • Cooking 15 minutes • Difficulty 1

1. Combine the beef with the soy sauce, apple juice, red pepper flakes, garlic, papaya, and tomatoes in a large nonreactive bowl. Use your hands to mix the ingredients for about 5 minutes to ensure all the spices are well absorbed. The heat from your hands will aid the tenderizing process. Let marinate for 2 hours.

2. Cook the noodles according to the instructions on the package. Drain and set aside.

3. Heat a wok or large frying pan over high heat and add the oil. Stir-fry the celery and ginger until aromatic, about 1 minute. Add the beef and the marinade. Stir occasionally until all the liquid has evaporated and the meat is tender, about 5 minutes.

4. Add the spinach and noodles. Stir-fry for another 2 minutes. Serve hot.

STICKY SIRLOIN STEAKS with cellophane noodles

12	ounces (350 g) gluten-free cellophane noodles
4	(8-ounce/250-g) rump or sirloin steaks
1/4	cup (60 ml) dark soy sauce
4	tablespoons (60 ml) Thai sweet chilli sauce
1	tablespoon peeled fresh ginger
2	cloves garlic, peeled
1/2	cup (60 g) cashew nuts
1	dried chili, crumbled
2	tablespoons peanut oil
2	carrots, cut into matchsticks
1	red bell pepper (capsicum), seeded and thinly sliced
	Handful fresh cilantro (coriander) leaves

Serves 4 • Preparation 10 minutes + 15 minutes to marinate • Cooking 15–20 minutes • Difficulty 1

1. Prepare the noodles according to the instructions on the package. Drain and refresh under cold running water. Drain again and set aside.

2. Marinate the steak in a bowl with the soy and sweet chilli sauces for 15 minutes.

3. Chop the ginger, garlic, cashews and chilli in a small food processor (or pound in a pestle and mortar) to form a paste. Set aside.

4. Heat a grill pan (griddle) or frying pan until very hot. Add the steaks, well coated in the marinade, and cook to your liking; 3–4 minutes each side for medium rare. Set aside.

5. Heat the peanut oil in a wok or frying pan over medium-high heat and fry the cashew paste for 1 minute. Add the carrots, bell pepper, and a splash of water and stir-fry for 2 minutes. Add the noodles and cilantro and stir well. Serve the noodles hot with the sticky beef.

BEEF & CHESTNUT stew

Serves 4 • Preparation 20 minutes • Cooking 2¼ hours
Difficulty 1

3	tablespoons all-purpose (plain) flour	2	sprigs thyme
	Salt and freshly ground black pepper	1	cup (250 ml) dry red wine
1¼	pounds (600 g) beef (braising or chuck steak), cut into cubes	1¼	cups (300 ml) beef stock
		2	carrots, sliced
2	tablespoons extra-virgin olive oil	8	ounces (250 g) cooked, peeled chestnuts, freshly roasted or vacuum packed
2	onions, chopped		

1. Season the flour generously with salt and pepper. Sprinkle over the beef, turning to coat. Heat the oil in a deep saucepan over high heat. Add the beef and sauté until browned, 8–10 minutes.

2. Add the onions and sauté until they start to brown, 4–5 minutes. Add the thyme, wine, and stock. Bring to a boil, then decrease the heat, cover, and simmer for 1 hour.

3. Add the carrots and chestnuts, season with salt and pepper, and simmer until the meat is very tender, about 1 more hour. Serve hot with rice or potatoes.

BEEF & VEGGIE stew

Serves 4–6 • Preparation 15 minutes • Cooking 2¾ hours
Difficulty 1

⅓	cup (90 ml) extra-virgin olive oil	1½	pounds (750 g) beef chuck, cubed
2	cloves garlic, 1 onion, 1 carrot, 1 stalk celery, all finely chopped		Salt and freshly ground black pepper
		1	cup (250 ml) red wine
4	medium tomatoes, peeled and chopped	2	cups (500 ml) beef stock
1	tablespoon mixed herbs (sage, parsley, oregano, rosemary, thyme), chopped	1¼	pounds (600 g) potatoes, peeled and cut in bite-size chunks

1. Heat the oil in a large, heavy-bottomed pan over medium heat. Add the chopped vegetables and herbs. Sauté until softened, about 5 minutes.

2. Remove any little pieces of fat from the meat. Add the meat to the pan, season with salt and pepper, and cook until brown. Pour in the wine and cook until it evaporates. Cover the pan and simmer for about 2 hours, gradually adding the stock. Stir frequently, to stop the meat from sticking to the pan.

3. Add the potatoes and simmer until tender, 30–45 minutes. Serve hot.

SHEPHERD'S pie

Serves 4 • Preparation 15 minutes • Cooking about 1 hour
Difficulty 1

6	medium potatoes, cut into chunks	3	tablespoons tomato paste (concentrate)
2	tablespoons butter	2–3	tablespoons Worcestershire sauce
3	tablespoons milk		
2	tablespoons extra-virgin olive oil	3	tablespoons ketchup
			Salt and freshly ground white pepper
1	large onion, minced		
1	pound (500 g) ground (minced) lamb	1	tablespoon chopped fresh parsley, to garnish

1. Boil the potatoes until tender, 15–20 minutes. Drain and mash with the butter and milk.

2. Heat the oil in a frying pan over medium heat. Add the onion and sauté until softened, 3–4 minutes. Add the lamb and sauté until browned, 4–5 minutes. Stir in the tomato paste, Worcestershire sauce, and ketchup. Season with salt and white pepper, and simmer on low heat for 15 minutes.

3. Preheat the oven to 375°F (190°C/gas 5). Spoon the lamb mixture into an ovenproof dish and top with the mashed potatoes. Bake for 25–30 minutes, until golden brown. Serve hot, garnished with the parsley.

ROAST LAMB Italian-style

Serves 4–6 • Preparation 15 minutes • Cooking about 1 hour
Difficulty 1

1	(4-pound/2-kg) shoulder of lamb (with some loin attached), bone in	¼	cup (120 ml) extra-virgin olive oil
			Salt and freshly ground black pepper
3	cloves garlic, peeled and cut in half	2	pounds (1 kg) roasting potatoes, peeled and cut into large chunks
4–6	sprigs fresh rosemary		

1. Preheat the oven to 350°F (180°C/gas 4).

2. Put the lamb in a large ovenproof dish. Use the point of a sharp knife to make small incisions in the meat and push the pieces of garlic in. Close the meat around it. Sprinkle with the rosemary. Drizzle with the oil. Season with salt and pepper. Place in the oven and begin roasting.

3. Arrange the potatoes around the meat after it has been in the oven for about 20 minutes. The meat should take about 1 hour to cook, while the potatoes will need only about 40 minutes.

4. Baste the meat with the cooking juices 2 or 3 times during roasting and turn the potatoes so that they are evenly browned.

5. Serve hot.

POTATO & ONION soufflés

3 pounds (1.5 kg) potatoes
6 large onions, sliced
1 tablespoon extra-virgin olive oil
8 tablespoons (120 g) butter
1 cup (250 ml) dry white wine
$1/2$ cup (120 ml) vegetable stock
   Freshly ground sea salt and black pepper
$1^1/4$ cups (300 ml) milk
3 large eggs, beaten
1 cup (120 g) freshly grated Parmesan cheese
1 cup (120 g) freshly grated Gruyère cheese
2 tablespoons almond meal

Serves 6-8 • Preparation 30 minutes • Cooking about 1 hour • Difficulty 1

1. Cook the potatoes in their skins in a pot of salted, boiling water until tender, 20–25 minutes. Drain, slip off the skins and mash.

2. Combine the onions, oil, 4 tablespoons of butter, wine, stock, salt, and pepper in a saucepan, cover, and simmer until the onions are soft and golden, about 35 minutes.

3. Heat the milk in a saucepan. Stir in the potatoes and 3 tablespoons of butter until smooth. Let cool for 10 minutes.

4. Preheat the oven to 350°F (180°C/gas 4).

5. Combine the potato purée with the eggs, salt, and pepper. Stir in the Parmesan (reserving 2 tablespoons).

6. Butter six to eight ramekins and spread with an even layer of potato (use half the potato). Spoon in the onions. Sprinkle with the Gruyère and cover with the remaining potatoes. Finish with the almond meal and Parmesan.

7. Bake for 20-25 minutes, until golden brown. Serve hot.

If you liked this recipe, you will love these as well.

CHEESE & VEGETABLE
clafoutis

BAKED POTATOES
with spicy cottage cheese

POTATO & CABBAGE
bake

SPINACH, CRANBERRY & ALMOND pilaf

1½	cups (300 g) basmati rice
2	tablespoons peanut oil
1	onion, finely chopped
1	clove garlic, finely chopped
1	cinnamon stick
¼	teaspoon ground nutmeg
	Pinch of ground cloves
1	teaspoon finely grated unwaxed orange zest
3	cups (750 ml) chicken stock, boiling
1	teaspoon saffron threads, infused in 2 tablespoons hot water
1½	cups (75 g) baby spinach
¼	cup (45 g) dried cranberries
½	cup (80 g) almonds, coarsely chopped

Serves 4–6 • Preparation 30 minutes + 1 hour to soak • Cooking 25–30 minutes • Difficulty 1

1. Put the rice in a medium bowl and cover with cold water. Leave to soak for 1 hour. Drain and rinse under cold water until water almost runs clear.

2. Heat the oil in a medium saucepan over medium heat. Add the onion and garlic and sauté until softened, 3–4 minutes. Add the cinnamon, nutmeg, and cloves and sauté until fragrant, about 1 minute.

3. Add the rice and orange zest and stir to coat the rice, about 2 minutes. Pour in the stock and saffron mixture and bring to a boil. Cover, decrease the heat to low, and simmer until the rice is almost tender, about 20 minutes.

4. Remove from the heat, add the spinach, cranberries, and almonds. Cover and set aside for 5 minutes to rest.

5. Stir well, and serve hot.

LEBANESE rice & lentils

1 cup (200 g) basmati rice

1¹/₂ cups (150 g) small brown lentils

3 tablespoons extra-virgin olive oil

1 teaspoon butter

1 large onion, finely chopped

1 teaspoon finely grated fresh ginger

1 green chili, seeded and finely chopped

1 teaspoon ground cinnamon

2 cloves

1 teaspoon freshly ground black pepper

1 teaspoon ground allspice

1 bay leaf

2 cups (500 ml) water

1 teaspoon salt

3 scallions (spring onions), sliced on the diagonal

Serves 4 • Preparation 20 minutes + 1 hour to soak • Cooking 35–40 minutes • Difficulty 2

1. Put the rice in a medium bowl and cover with cold water. Leave to soak for 1 hour. Drain and rinse under cold water until water almost runs clean.

2. Put the lentils in a saucepan and cover with 4 cups (1 liter) of water. Bring to a boil over medium heat. Decrease the heat to low, partially cover, and simmer until the lentils are beginning to soften, 15–20 minutes. Drain and set aside.

3. Heat the oil and butter in a pot over medium heat. Add the onion, ginger, and chili and sauté until softened and lightly colored, 3–4 minutes. Add the cinnamon, cloves, black pepper, allspice, and bay leaf, and cook for 2 more minutes.

4. Stir in the rice and lentils. Pour in the water. Add the salt, stir well, and cover with a tight-fitting lid. Bring to a boil over medium heat and keep bubbling for 3 minutes.

5. Decrease the heat to low and simmer until the rice and lentils are tender and all the liquid has been absorbed, about 10 minutes. Stir in the scallions and serve hot.

A clafoutis is a baked French dessert, traditionally made with black cherries, sugar, and cream. In this recipe we have adapted the technique to make a savory clafoutis with bread, vegetables, and cheese.

This recipe includes six slices of gluten-free bread. You can either use store-bought gluten-free bread or prepare our recipe on page 38.

CHEESE & VEGETABLE clafoutis

¹/₄	cup (60 ml) extra-virgin olive oil
1	shallot, finely chopped
2	zucchini (courgettes), cut into small cubes
2	carrots, cut into small cubes
	Small bunch asparagus tips, chopped
1	cup (150 g) frozen peas
	Sea salt flakes
6	slices gluten-free bread
1	teaspoon sweet paprika
1	tablespoon cornstarch (cornflour)
¹/₃	cup (90 ml) milk
¹/₃	cup (90 ml) heavy (double) cream
2	large eggs, lightly beaten
5	ounces (150 g) Brie cheese, thinly sliced
1	cup (120 g) freshly grated Parmesan cheese

Serves 4–6 • Preparation 20 minutes • Cooking 30–35 minutes
Difficulty 2

1. Preheat the oven to 350°F (180°C/gas 4).

2. Heat the oil in a large frying pan over medium heat. Add the shallot and sauté until softened, 3–4 minutes. Add the zucchini, carrots, asparagus, and peas and cook for 5 minutes. Season with the salt.

3. Oil two baking sheets. Place the gluten-free bread on the baking sheets and dust with the paprika. Toast in the oven until lightly browned. Remove and set aside.

4. Whisk the cornstarch and milk in a small bowl. Heat the cream and eggs in a saucepan over medium heat, stirring constantly. Add the milk mixture and stir until thickened.

5. Cover the base of a large baking dish with the toast and top with the Brie. Spoon the vegetables over the top. Pour in the sauce and sprinkle with the Parmesan. Bake for 20–25 minutes, until the vegetables are tender. Serve hot.

If you liked this recipe, you will love these as well.

POTATO & ONION
soufflés

VEGETABLES
al cartoccio

POTATO & CABBAGE
bake

BAKED POTATOES with spicy cottage cheese

6	medium potatoes
12	ounces (350 g) cottage cheese
2	teaspoons tomato paste (concentrate)
1	teaspoon cumin seeds
1	teaspoon ground coriander
1	teaspoon red pepper flakes
	Freshly ground sea salt and black pepper
1	tablespoon extra-virgin olive oil
$1/2$	teaspoon mixed onion and mustard seeds
3	tablespoons water
	Chopped fresh chives, to serve

Serves 6 • Preparation 15 minutes • Cooking 1 hour • Difficulty 1

1. Preheat the oven to 350°F (180°C/gas 4).

2. Scrub the potatoes under cold running water. Pat dry and cut a slit in the top of each one. Prick with a fork, then wrap each potato in a piece of aluminum foil. Bake until tender, about 1 hour.

3. Place the cottage cheese in a heatproof bowl and set aside. Place the tomato paste, cumin, coriander, red pepper flakes, salt, and pepper in another bowl.

4. Heat the oil in a small saucepan and sauté the onion and mustard seeds for 1 minute. Add the tomato paste mixture and water to the saucepan and mix well. Cook for 1 minute, then pour the spicy tomato mixture into the cottage cheese. Mix well.

5. Unwrap the potatoes and cut open. Divide the cottage cheese mixture equally among them. Garnish with the chives, and serve hot.

BAKED TOMATOES with parmesan risotto

8   medium tomatoes
4   tablespoons (60 g) butter
1   tablespoon very finely chopped onion
1   cup (200 g) Arborio rice
2   cups (500 ml) boiling vegetable stock
$^1\!/_2$ cup (60 g) freshly grated Parmesan cheese
    Freshly ground sea salt and black pepper
2   large eggs
1   cup (125 g) almond meal

Serves 4 • Preparation 30 minutes • Cooking 50–60 minutes
Difficulty 2

1. Preheat the oven to 400°F (200°C/gas 6). Butter an ovenproof dish into which the tomatoes will fit snugly.

2. Cut the tops off the tomatoes. Set aside. Use a teaspoon to hollow out and discard the flesh and seeds.

3. Heat 2 tablespoons of butter in a frying pan over medium heat. Add the onion and sauté until softened, 3–4 minutes. Add the rice, and cook for 2 minutes, stirring constantly. Begin stirring in the stock, $^1\!/_2$ cup (120 ml) at a time. Cook and stir until each addition has been absorbed, and the rice is tender, 15–18 minutes. Stir in the cheese. Season with salt and pepper. Stuff the tomatoes with the risotto and top each one neatly with its lid.

4. Beat the eggs lightly in a bowl and dip the stuffed tomatoes into the beaten egg. Coat with the almond meal.

5. Place the tomatoes in the prepared baking dish. Top each tomato with a flake of the remaining butter. Bake until golden, 25–30 minutes. Serve hot or at room temperature.

Al cartoccio is an Italian cooking technique in which the food is wrapped in parchment paper or aluminum foil and baked in the oven until ready. Food cooked in this way is tender and moist, with all its natural flavors intact. It is also a fun way to serve food; bring the parcel of vegetables to the table and unwrap before your guests' eyes.

VEGETABLES al cartoccio

14	ounces (400 g) Brussels sprouts, halved
1	small head broccoli, cut into florets
16	cherry tomatoes
8	baby carrots, tops removed
2	celery sticks, tough outer ridges removed and discarded, coarsely chopped
2	small leeks, sliced
2	cloves garlic, finely chopped
1	tablespoon finely chopped fresh rosemary
1	tablespoon finely chopped fresh parsley
1	tablespoon finely chopped fresh thyme
1	tablespoon finely chopped fresh oregano
	Freshly ground sea salt and black pepper
5	tablespoons (75 ml) extra-virgin olive oil

Serves 4–6 • Preparation 15 minutes • Cooking 40 minutes • Difficulty 1

1. Preheat the oven to 350°F (180°C/gas 4).

2. Place all the vegetables in a large bowl. Add the garlic, rosemary, parsley, thyme, and oregano. Season with salt and pepper and drizzle with the oil. Mix well.

3. Line a large roasting pan with a sheet of parchment paper or aluminum foil large enough to fold over all the vegetables. Place the vegetable mixture in the parchment and close the paper over, folding to seal well. Secure the parcel with staples.

4. Bake for about 40 minutes, until the vegetables are tender.

5. Remove from the oven and transfer the parcel intact to a large serving dish. Open the parchment paper package at the table, and serve at once.

If you liked this recipe, you will love these as well.

CHEESE & VEGETABLE
clafoutis

ROASTED MUSHROOMS
with spinach & rice stuffing

POTATO & CABBAGE
bake

ROMAN-STYLE spinach

Serves 6 • Preparation 20 minutes + 30 minutes to soak
Cooking 6 minutes • Difficulty 1

4	tablespoons raisins	6	tablespoons pine nuts
3	tablespoons extra-virgin olive oil	3	pounds (1.5 kg) tender young spinach leaves
2	cloves garlic, finely chopped		Freshly ground sea salt and black pepper

1. Plump the raisins in cold water for 30 minutes. Drain well.

2. Heat the oil in a large frying pan over high heat. Add the garlic and pine nuts and sauté for 1 minute. Add the spinach and raisins and sauté for 5 minutes.

3. Season with salt and pepper, and serve hot.

GARLIC mash

Serves 4-6 • Preparation 15 minutes • Cooking 15-20 minutes • Difficulty 1

2	pounds (1 kg) potatoes, peeled and quartered	3	cloves garlic, finely chopped
1/3	cup (90) ml extra-virgin olive oil		Sea salt flakes
1/3	cup (90 ml) freshly squeezed lemon juice	3	tablespoons finely chopped fresh mint

1. Cook the potatoes in a large pot of salted boiling water until tender, 15-20 minutes.

2. Drain well, transfer to a large bowl, and mash until smooth. Add the oil, lemon juice, garlic, and salt and stir until well blended.

3. Sprinkle with the mint, and serve warm.

WILD MUSHROOM fricassée

Serves 4 • Preparation 15 minutes • Cooking 15-20 minutes Difficulty 1

1 1/2	pounds (750 g) mixed wild mushrooms		sweet paprika
2	tablespoons extra-virgin olive oil	2	ounces (50 g) sun-dried tomatoes in oil, chopped
2	shallots, sliced	4	tablespoons finely chopped fresh parsley
2	cloves garlic, minced		
2	tablespoons butter	1	cup (250 ml) sour cream
1 1/2	teaspoons salt		Freshly ground sea salt and black pepper
2/3	cup (150 ml) dry sherry		
1	teaspoon smoked		

1. Halve or quarter the mushrooms so that they are all more or less the same size.

2. Heat the oil in a large frying pan over medium heat. Add the shallots and sauté until softened but not colored, 3-4 minutes. Stir in the garlic and butter. Increase the heat to high and add all the mushrooms to the pan. Cover, and simmer over medium heat until they are beginning to soften, 5-6 minutes.

3. Add the salt, sherry, and paprika. Stir gently and bring to a boil. Cover the pan and simmer over low heat for 5 more minutes. Stir in the sun-dried tomatoes, 2 tablespoons of parsley, and the sour cream. Simmer for 2-3 minutes. Sprinkle with the remaining parsley and serve hot.

ASIAN GREENS with oyster sauce

Serves 4 • Preparation 15 minutes • Cooking 10 minutes Difficulty 1

2	tablespoons peanut oil	1/4	cup (60 ml) chicken stock
2	cloves garlic, thinly sliced	1	bunch Asian broccoli
1 1/2	cups (150 g) sliced fresh mushrooms, such as oyster or shiitake	1	bunch baby choi sum
		1	bunch baby bok choy
1/2	cup (120 ml) oyster sauce	2	cups (100 g) Chinese cabbage, coarsely chopped

1. Place a large saucepan of water on high heat and bring to a boil.

2. Heat the oil in a large wok or frying pan over medium-high heat. Add the garlic and mushrooms and sauté until golden brown, about 5 minutes.

3. Pour in the oyster sauce and chicken stock and bring to a boil. Decrease the heat to low and simmer until slightly reduced, 2-3 minutes.

4. Meanwhile, cook the broccoli in the boiling water for 1 minute. Add the choi sum and bok choy and cook for 2 more minutes. Add the cabbage and cook until just wilted, about 30 seconds. Drain well.

5. Add to the mushrooms in the pan and toss to combine and coat in the sauce. Serve hot.

ROASTED VEGETABLES
with pine nut & rice stuffing

4 medium to large tomatoes
4 small to medium bell peppers (capsicums), mixed colors
1½ cups (300 g) short-grain rice
4 tablespoons (60 ml) extra-virgin olive oil
1 large onion, finely chopped
2 cloves garlic, finely chopped
1 teaspoon dried oregano
5 tablespoons pine nuts
5 tablespoons golden raisins (sultanas)
4 tablespoons finely chopped fresh basil
3 tablespoons finely chopped fresh parsley
Freshly ground sea salt and black pepper

Serves 4-6 • Preparation 30 minutes • Cooking 50-65 minutes
Difficulty 2

1. Preheat the oven to 350°F (180°C/gas 4). Oil a baking dish.

2. Slice the tops off the tomatoes and set aside. Use a teaspoon to hollow them out, placing the flesh in a cup. Place the tomatoes upside down in a colander to drain.

3. Cut the tops off the bell peppers and remove the seeds. Reserve the tops. Trim the bottoms so they stand upright.

4. Bring a pot of lightly salted water to a boil over high heat. Add the rice and simmer until almost tender, 10-12 minutes. Drain and let cool in a large bowl.

5. Heat 2 tablespoons of oil in a large frying pan over medium heat. Add the onion, garlic, and oregano and sauté until softened, 3-4 minutes. Add the pine nuts and golden raisins and simmer for 5 minutes. Stir in the basil and parsley.

6. Add the sautéed mixture and the tomato flesh to the rice and mix well. Season with salt and pepper.

7. Stuff the vegetables with the mixture. Cover with the reserved tops. Arrange in the baking dish and drizzle with the remaining 2 tablespoons of oil.

8. Cover with aluminum foil and bake for 40-50 minutes, until the vegetables are tender. Serve hot.

ROASTED MUSHROOMS
with spinach & rice stuffing

Serves 4 • Preparation 30 minutes • Cooking 50 minutes • Difficulty 2

¹/₄ cup (45 g) golden raisins (sultanas)

1 cup (200 g) long-grain rice

1 cup (50 g) baby spinach, finely shredded

8 medium, firm mushrooms

1 onion, finely chopped

1 clove garlic, finely chopped

3 tablespoons extra-virgin olive oil

¹/₄ cup (45 g) pine nuts, toasted

1 tablespoon coarsely chopped fresh parsley

1 tablespoon coarsely chopped fresh cilantro (coriander)

1 teaspoon ground cumin

1 teaspoon ground coriander

Pinch of cinnamon

Freshly ground sea salt and black pepper

1. Bring a large pot of lightly salted water to a boil over high heat. Add the rice, return to a boil, then simmer over low heat until almost tender, 10–12 minutes.

2. Plump the raisins in hot water for 5 minutes. Drain. Preheat the oven to 400°F (200°C/gas 6).

3. Drain the rice and return to the pan. Add the spinach and mix well. Cover and let stand for 10 minutes.

4. Remove the stalks from the mushrooms and chop them. Sauté the chopped mushroom stalks, onion, and garlic in the oil in a large frying pan over medium heat until softened, 3–4 minutes.

5. Stir in the golden raisins, pine nuts, parsley, cilantro, cumin, coriander, and cinnamon. Season with salt and pepper. Stir in the spinach and rice.

6. Fill the mushroom caps with the mixture. Place in a baking dish. Bake for 30 minutes, until the mushrooms are tender. Serve hot.

This dish is hearty, comforting, and versatile. It goes beautifully with grilled or roasted fish and meats, but can also be served as part of a vegetarian spread, including salads and legume dishes.

POTATO & CABBAGE bake

2	pounds (1 kg) starchy (baking) potatoes, peeled
3	tablespoons extra-virgin olive oil
2	cloves garlic, finely chopped
12	ounces (350 g) Savoy cabbage, coarsely chopped
3	large eggs, beaten
1	teaspoon cumin seeds
1/2	cup (60 g) freshly grated Parmesan cheese
	Freshly ground sea salt and black pepper
5	ounces (150 g) mozzarella cheese, thinly sliced or grated

Serves 4-6 • Preparation 15 minutes • Cooking 60–75 minutes
Difficulty 1

1. Cook the potatoes in a large pot of salted boiling water until tender, 20–25 minutes. Drain well. Mash two-thirds of the potatoes. Cut the remaining potatoes into bite-size pieces. Place the potatoes in a bowl.

2. Preheat the oven to 350°F (180°C/gas 4). Grease a 10-inch (25-cm) baking pan.

3. Heat the oil in a large frying pan over medium heat. Add the garlic and cabbage and sauté until the cabbage is tender, 5–10 minutes. Add the cabbage to the potatoes and mix gently. Add the eggs, half the cumin, and Parmesan. Season with salt and pepper and mix well.

4. Spoon the mixture into the prepared pan and level the surface with the back of a spoon. Top with the mozzarella and sprinkle with the remaining cumin seeds.

5. Bake for 35–40 minutes, until golden brown. Serve hot.

If you liked this recipe, you will love these as well.

POTATO & ONION soufflés

BAKED POTATO with spicy cottage cheese

BAKED POTATO & SPINACH roll

BAKED POTATO & SPINACH roll

1	pound (500 g) starchy (baking) potatoes, peeled
5	cup (350 g) fresh spinach
5	ounces (150 g) ricotta cheese, drained
2	large egg yolks, lightly beaten
$1/2$	cup (60 g) freshly grated Parmesan cheese + extra, to sprinkle
$1/4$	teaspoon freshly grated nutmeg
	Freshly ground sea salt and black pepper
$2/3$	cup (100 g) fine polenta (stoneground cornmeal)
$1/4$	cup (60 g) butter
6	sage leaves

Serves 4 • Preparation 30 minutes + 1 hour to cool • Cooking 55–60 minutes • Difficulty 3

1. Cook the potatoes in a large pot of salted boiling water until tender, 20–25 minutes. Drain and mash in a large bowl.

2. Cook the spinach in salted boiling until tender, 4–5 minutes. Drain well and chop finely.

3. Mix the spinach, ricotta, 1 egg yolk, half the Parmesan, and the nutmeg in a bowl. Season with salt and pepper. Add the remaining egg yolk, remaining Parmesan, the polenta, and a pinch of salt to the bowl with the potatoes. Mix well.

4. Roll out the potato mixture on a sheet of parchment paper to $1/4$ inch (5 mm) thick. Spread with the spinach mixture, leaving a 1-inch (2.5-cm) border all around. Roll up using the paper to help you. Wrap the roll securely in the paper and seal the ends, tying with kitchen string.

5. Put the roll into a large casserole and cover with boiling water. Simmer for 20 minutes. Remove from the heat and drain. Let cool before unwrapping it, about 1 hour.

6. Preheat the oven to 400°F (200°C/gas 6). Melt the butter with the sage in a small saucepan over low heat.

7. Slice the roulade. Arrange in a baking dish. Drizzle with the butter mixture and sprinkle with extra Parmesan. Bake for 10 minutes, until slightly crisp on top. Serve hot.

LENTIL stew

2   red bell peppers (capsicums), halved and seeded

2   tablespoons extra-virgin olive oil + extra, to drizzle

1   large red onion, chopped

1   leek, thinly sliced

1   large carrot, cut into fine dice

1   teaspoon paprika

1   cup (175 g) Le Puy lentils

1   clove garlic, sliced

4   ripe tomatoes, peeled and chopped

3   sprigs fresh thyme + extra, to garnish

2   bay leaves

2   cups (500 ml) vegetable stock

1   tablespoon capers

12   pitted black olives

2   tablespoons coarsely chopped fresh parsley

2   tablespoons red wine vinegar

   Freshly ground sea salt and black pepper

   Squeeze of fresh lemon juice

Serves 4 • Preparation 30 minute • Cooking 50–55 minutes • Difficulty 2

1. Preheat an overhead broiler (grill). Broil the bell peppers skin-side up, until blackened, about 10 minutes. Place in a plastic bag and tie the top. When cool enough to handle, peel off the skin. Cut into strips and set aside.

2. Heat the oil in a large saucepan over low heat. Add the onion, leek, and carrot. Cover and simmer until softened, about 10 minutes. Stir in the paprika.

3. Rinse the lentils under cold water and add to the saucepan with the garlic, tomatoes, thyme, and bay leaves. Pour in enough of the stock to cover well. Increase the heat and bring to a boil, stirring frequently. Reduce the heat and simmer gently, uncovered and stirring often, until the lentils are tender but not mushy, 20–25 minutes.

4. Stir in the bell peppers, capers, olives, and parsley. Remove the bay leaves and thyme, and stir in the vinegar. Cook for 10 more minutes. Season with salt and pepper, lemon juice, and a drizzle of oil. Garnish with extra thyme and serve hot.

desserts

GLUTEN-FREE *citrus torte*

1   cup (200 g) sugar
1   cup (100 g) hazelnut meal
$^1/_3$ cup (30 g) quinoa flour
4   large eggs
$^1/_4$ cup (60 ml) extra-virgin olive oil
2   tablespoons finely grated unwaxed lemon zest
1   tablespoon freshly squeezed lemon juice
1   tablespoon freshly squeezed orange juice
$^1/_4$ teaspoon sea salt flakes
    Thinly sliced oranges or lemons, caramelized, to serve (optional)
    Confectioners' (icing) sugar, to dust

Serves 4 • Preparation 25 minutes • Cooking 30–35 minutes
Difficulty 2

1. Preheat the oven to 350°F (180°C/gas 4). Line the base of a 9-inch (23-cm) springform pan with parchment paper.

2. Combine $^1/_3$ cup of the sugar with the hazelnut meal and quinoa flour in a bowl.

3. Beat $^1/_3$ cup of sugar of the remaining sugar with the egg yolks in a bowl with an electric mixer on medium speed until thick and pale, about 5 minutes. Beat in the oil, lemon zest and citrus juices. Fold in the hazelnut flour mixture.

4. Beat the egg whites and salt in a bowl until frothy. Beat in the remaining sugar on high speed until stiff peaks form. Fold one third of the egg white mixture into the batter. Gently fold in the remaining egg-white mixture in two batches. Spoon the batter into the prepared pan.

5. Bake for 30–35 minutes, until golden. Let cool in the pan for 10 minutes, then release the pan sides and let cool completely. Dust with confectioners' sugar and top with the caramelized oranges or lemons, if liked. Slice and serve.

If you liked this recipe, you will love these as well.

LEMON macarons

CHILLED CHOCOLATE ORANGE cake

LEMON cheesecake

You can vary these cookies by using milk or white chocolate chips instead of the dark chocolate. You could also replace the toasted pecans with the same quantity of toasted walnut pieces.

CHOCOLATE CHIP cookies

1/2	cup butter, softened
1/4	cup (60 ml) coconut oil, softened
1	cup (200 g) firmly packed light brown sugar
2	teaspoons vanilla extract (essence)
2	large eggs
1/2	teaspoon baking soda (bicarbonate of soda)
1/2	teaspoon sea salt flakes
3	cups (300 g) almond meal
1 1/3	cups (245 g) dark chocolate
2/3	cup (80 g) toasted pecans

Makes 24 • Preparation 20 minutes + 30 minutes to chill • Cooking 11–13 minutes • Difficulty 1

1. Preheat the oven to 350°F (180°C/gas 4). Line two large baking sheets with parchment paper.

2. Beat the butter, coconut oil, and brown sugar in a bowl until creamy. Add the vanilla and eggs, beating until just combined.

3. Beat in the baking soda and salt. Gradually beat in the almond meal. Fold in the chocolate chips and pecans by hand. Cover the bowl with plastic wrap (cling film) and chill for 30 minutes.

4. Scoop out tablespoons of dough and place on the baking sheets, spacing about 2 inches (5 cm) apart.

5. Bake for 11–13 minutes, until golden brown. Let cool on the baking sheets for 2–3 minutes, then transfer to a wire rack and let cool completely.

If you liked this recipe, you will love these as well.

CHOCOLATE CARAMEL
macaroons

CHOCOLATE meringues

CHOCOLATE ALMOND
torte

CELEBRATION cupcakes

Cupcakes

½	cup (60 g) amaranth flour
¾	cup (125 g) rice flour
1	tablespoon (8 g) xanthan gum
1	teaspoon baking soda (bicarbonate of soda)
1	teaspoon ground cinnamon
¼	teaspoon ground cloves
⅛	teaspoon salt
	large eggs
¾	cup (150 g) sugar
½	cup (120 ml) vegetable oil
¼	cup (60 ml) water
¾	cup (135 g) tart apple, such as Granny Smith, peeled, cored, and grated
½	cup (60 g) walnuts, coarsely chopped

Cream Cheese Frosting

⅔	cup (150 g) cream cheese, softened
½	teaspoon finely grated unwaxed lemon zest
⅔	cup (100 g) confectioners' (icing) sugar
1	tablespoon fresh lemon juice
	Sugar flowers, to decorate

Makes 12 • Preparation 30 minutes • Cooking 25–30 minutes
Difficulty 2

Cupcakes

1. Preheat the oven to 325°F (170°C/gas 3). Line a 12-cup muffin pan with paper liners.

2. Combine both flours, xanthan gum, baking soda, cinnamon, cloves, and salt in a bowl. Whisk the eggs in a bowl with an electric mixer on medium-high speed until frothy. Add the sugar, oil, and water and whisk until incorporated. With the mixer on low speed, add the mixed dry ingredients. Stir in the apple and walnuts by hand. Spoon the batter evenly into the prepared cups.

3. Bake for 25–30 minutes, until golden brown and firm to the touch. Transfer the pan to a wire rack to cool.

Cream Cheese Frosting

1. Beat the cream cheese and lemon zest in a bowl using an electric mixer on medium speed until creamy. Add the confectioners' sugar, and lemon juice, beating until combined.

2. Spread the frosting each cupcake. Top with the flowers.

BIRTHDAY cupcakes

Cupcakes

2	cups (250 g) finely ground pecans
1¼	cups (250 g) sugar
¼	cup (30 g) unsweetened cocoa powder, sifted
1	teaspoon baking powder
1	teaspoon ground cinnamon
⅛	teaspoon salt
4	large eggs
½	cup (120 ml) melted butter
1	teaspoon vanilla extract
1	teaspoon finely grated unwaxed orange zest

Frosting

4	ounces (120 g) dark chocolate, coarsely chopped
¼	cup (60 ml) light (single) cream
1½	cups (225 g) confectioners' (icing) sugar
2	tablespoons water
	Numbered candles

Makes 12 • Preparation 30 minutes • Cooking 25–30 minutes
Difficulty 2

Cupcakes

1. Preheat the oven to 325°F (170°C/gas 3). Line a 12-cup muffin pan with paper liners.

2. Mix the pecans, sugar, cocoa, baking powder, cinnamon, and salt in a bowl. Whisk the eggs, butter, vanilla, and orange zest in another bowl, then beat into the pecan mixture. Spoon the batter evenly into the prepared cups.

3. Bake for 25–30 minutes, until golden brown and firm to the touch. Transfer the pan to a wire rack to cool.

Frosting

1. Melt the chocolate and cream in a double boiler over barely simmering water until smooth. Set aside to cool and thicken. Spread over the cupcakes.

2. Stir the confectioners' sugar and water in a small bowl until smooth. Spoon into a small plastic bag and snip off the corner. Pipe a decorative border around the edges of the cupcakes. Arrange the candles in one cupcake. Pipe the birthday age on the remaining cupcakes.

A macaron is a French meringue-like cookie made with egg white, sugar, almond meal, and other flavorings and colorings. Macarons are usually filled and stuck together in pairs. Like all meringues, they are great for people with gluten intolerance.

CHOCOLATE CARAMEL macarons

1½ cups (225 g) confectioners' (icing) sugar
1 cup (100 g) almond meal
¼ cup (30 g) unsweetened cocoa powder
¼ teaspoon fine salt
3 large egg whites
1¼ cups (250 g) sugar
¼ cup (60 ml) water
2 ounces (60 g) bittersweet chocolate, chopped

Makes 12–15 • Preparation 40 minutes + 30 minutes to dry • Cooking 25–30 minutes • Difficulty 3

1. Line three large baking sheets with parchment paper.

2. Whisk the confectioners' sugar, almond flour, cocoa, and salt in a bowl.

3. Beat the egg whites in a bowl with an electric mixer on medium speed until pale and frothy. Keep beating, slowly adding ½ cup of confectioners' sugar, until stiff peaks form. Fold in the almond mixture in batches.

4. Spoon the batter into a pastry bag. Pipe 1-inch (2.5-cm) rounds of batter about 1 inch (2.5 cm) inch apart on the prepared baking sheets. Let sit at room temperature for 30 minutes until the tops of the macarons are dry.

5. Preheat the oven to 350°F (180°C/gas 4). Bake the macarons for 10–12 minutes, until puffed and firm.

6. Transfer the baking sheets to wire racks to cool completely. When cool, remove from the sheets.

7. Combine the remaining 1 cup of confectioners' sugar with the water in a clean dry frying pan over medium heat. Cook, swirling the pan occasionally, until the sugar melts and turns a deep reddish brown, about 15 minutes.

8. Working quickly, spoon the caramel over half the macarons and sandwich together with the remaining macarons.

9. Melt the chocolate in a in the microwave. Using a fork, drizzle the cookies with the melted chocolate. Let set at room temperature or in the refrigerator before serving.

RASPBERRY macaroons

Makes 10–12 • Preparation 40 minutes + 30 minutes to dry
Cooking 12–15 minutes • Difficulty 3

4	large egg whites	1	cup (150 g) finely ground almonds
2	cups (300 g) confectioners' (icing) sugar	1/2	cup (120 g) mascarpone cheese
	Few drops red food coloring	6	tablespoons raspberry preserves (jam)

1. Line three baking sheets with parchment paper.

2. Beat the egg whites in a bowl with an electric mixer on medium speed until frothy. Gradually beat in the confectioners' sugar until thick and glossy. Add the red food coloring. Fold in the almonds.

3. Transfer to a piping bag and pipe out 40 circles about 2 inches (5 cm) in diameter on the baking sheets, spacing 1 inch (2.5 cm) apart. Let sit at room temperature until the tops dry, about 30 minutes.

4. Preheat the oven to 350°F (180°C/gas 4). Bake for 12–15 minutes, until puffed and firm. Let cool completely on the baking sheets.

5. Beat the mascarpone and raspberry preserves in a bowl. Sandwich the macarons together with this mixture.

CRANBERRY meringues

Makes 12–15 • Preparation 15 minutes + 12 hours to dry out
Cooking 40–50 minutes • Difficulty 1

4	large egg whites	1/4	cup (45 g) shelled pistachios, chopped
1 1/4	cups (250 g) superfine (caster) sugar	2/3	cup (150 ml) heavy (double) cream
1/2	cup (90 g) dried cranberries		

1. Preheat the oven to 250°F (120°C/gas 1). Line a large baking sheet with parchment paper.

2. Beat the egg whites in a large bowl with an electric mixer on medium speed until frothy. Gradually beat in the sugar until thick and glossy. Use a large metal spoon to fold in the cranberries.

3. Drop tablespoons of the meringue onto the prepared baking sheet, spacing well. Sprinkle with the pistachios.

4. Bake for 40–50 minutes, until crisp and dry. Turn off the oven and leave to dry out overnight.

5. Beat the cream into soft peaks and serve a dollop with each meringue.

CHOCOLATE meringues

Makes 12 • Preparation 30 minutes + overnight to dry out
Cooking 30 minutes • Difficulty 2

Meringues

4	ounces (120 g) dark chocolate	1/3	cup (50 g) confectioners' (icing) sugar
3	large egg whites	2	tablespoons boiling water
3/4	cup (150 g) superfine (caster) sugar	3/4	cup (180 ml) heavy (double) double cream
Filling		2	ounces (60 g) dark chocolate, to decorate
2	tablespoons cocoa		

Meringues

1. Preheat the oven to 300°F (150°C/gas 2). Line two large baking sheets with parchment paper. Melt the chocolate in the microwave. Set aside to cool.

2. Beat the egg whites in a bowl until frothy. Beat in the sugar until thick and glossy. Fold in the chocolate.

3. Spoon the mixture onto the baking sheets into 24 meringues, spacing evenly. Bake for 30 minutes. Turn off the oven and let dry out overnight.

Filling

1. Mix the cocoa, sugar, and water until smooth. Let cool 30 minutes. Beat the cream until stiff. Mix in the chocolate. Sandwich the meringues with the filling.

LEMON macarons

Makes 18 • Preparation 45 minutes + 30 minutes to dry
Cooking 12–15 minutes • Difficulty 3

2	cups (300 g) confectioners' (icing) sugar	1/3	cup (75 g) superfine (caster) sugar
1	cup (150 g) almond meal	1	teaspoon lemon extract
3	large egg whites		Yellow food coloring
1/8	teaspoon salt	2/3	cup (150 g) butter, softened

1. Line three baking sheets with parchment paper.

2. Chop 1 1/3 cups (200 g) confectioners' sugar and almonds in a food processor, then sift into a bowl.

3. Beat the egg whites and salt in a bowl until frothy. Gradually beat in the sugar until thick and glossy. Stir in half the lemon extract and yellow food coloring. Fold the almond mixture into the meringue.

4. Transfer to a piping bag and pipe out 36 small circles , spacing 1 inch (2.5 cm) apart. Let sit at room temperature until the tops dry, about 30 minutes.

5. Preheat the oven to 350°F (180°C/gas 4). Bake for 12–15 minutes, until puffed and firm. Let cool completely on the baking sheets.

6. Beat the butter and remaining 2/3 cup (100 g) confectioners' sugar in a bowl with the remaining lemon extract and yellow food coloring. Sandwich the macarons together with this mixture.

PISTACHIO torte

1½ cups (225 g) pistachios
1 cup (200 g) sugar
3 large eggs, separated
2 tablespoons finely grated lemon zest
1 teaspoon baking powder
½ teaspoon baking soda (bicarbonate of soda)
¼ teaspoon salt
½ cup (120 ml) heavy (double) cream
1 tablespoon confectioners' (icing) sugar

Serves 8 • Preparation 30 minutes • Cooking 25-35 minutes • Difficulty 1

1. Preheat the oven to 350°F (180°C/gas 4). Lightly grease a 9-inch (23-cm) springform pan.

2. Plunge the pistachios into a saucepan of boiling water for 30 seconds. Drain well. Rub dry with a clean kitchen towel to remove the inner skins. Place the pistachios and sugar in a food processor and chop finely.

3. Transfer to a large bowl and stir in the egg yolks, lemon zest, baking powder, baking soda, and salt.

4. Beat the egg whites in a medium bowl with an electric mixer at high speed until stiff peaks form. Use a large rubber spatula to fold them into the batter. Spoon the batter into the prepared pan.

5. Bake for 25–35 minutes, until a toothpick inserted into the center comes out clean. Cool the cake in the pan for 10 minutes. Loosen and remove the pan sides and let the cake cool completely on a rack.

6. Beat the cream and confectioners' sugar in a medium bowl until thick. Put a dollop of cream on each slice, and serve.

CHOCOLATE HAZELNUT torte

10 ounces (300 g) dark chocolate, coarsely chopped

3/4 cup (180 g) butter, chopped

1 1/2 teaspoons vanilla extract (essence)

6 large eggs

1 cup (200 g) firmly packed dark brown sugar

1 teaspoon finely grated unwaxed orange zest

1 cup (100 g) ground hazelnuts

Confectioner's sugar, to dust

Serves 8–10 • Preparation 30 minutes • Cooking 35–40 minutes
Difficulty 1

1. Preheat the oven to 325°F (170°C/gas 3). Lightly grease a 9-inch (23-cm) springform cake pan and line the base and sides with parchment paper.

2. Melt the chocolate, butter, and vanilla in a double boiler over barely simmering water, stirring occasionally until smooth. Remove from the heat and set aside to cool.

3. Beat the egg yolks, brown sugar, and orange zest in a large bowl with an electric mixer on medium speed until pale and thick. Add the melted chocolate and stir to combine.

4. Beat the egg whites in a separate bowl until soft peaks form. Add a third of the whites to the yolk mixture and stir to combine, and then fold in the remaining whites. Fold in the ground hazelnuts. Spoon the batter into the prepared pan and cover with aluminum foil.

5. Bake for 35–40 minutes, until a skewer comes out clean when tested. Remove the foil and leave to cool for 10 minutes. Turn out onto a wire rack and let cool completely.

6. Dust with confectioners' sugar just before serving.

This chocolatey torte falls somewhere between a brownie and a cake. It can also be prepared ahead of time and chilled until ready to serve.

CHOCOLATE PECAN torte

Torte

5	tablespoons (75 g) unsalted butter
6	ounces (180 g) dark chocolate
1	cup (120 g) pecans
1/2	cup (90 g) dark chocolate chips
6	large eggs
1	teaspoon vanilla extract (essence)
1	cup (200 g) sugar
	Pinch of sea salt flakes

To Serve

3	tablespoons brown sugar
	Finely grated zest of 1 unwaxed lemon
1/4	cup (60 ml) freshly squeezed lemon juice
2	cups (300 g) strawberries, halved
2	cups (300 g) raspberries
	Lightly sweetened whipped cream

Serves 6–8 • Preparation 30 minutes • Cooking 40–45 minutes
Difficulty 1

Torte

1. Preheat the oven to 350°F (180°C/gas 4). Line a 9-inch (23-cm) springform pan with parchment paper.

2. Melt the chocolate and butter in a double boiler over barely simmering water.

3. Chop the pecans finely in a food processor. Add the eggs, vanilla, sugar, salt, melted chocolate mixture, and chocolate chips, blending until smooth.

4. Pour the batter into the prepared pan. Bake for 40–45 minutes, until a toothpick inserted into the center comes out clean. Let cool completely in the pan.

To Serve

1. Combine the brown sugar, lemon zest, and juice in a bowl. Add the berries and toss gently. Spoon over the cake. Slice and serve with the whipped cream.

If you liked this recipe, you will love these as well.

PISTACHIO
torte

CHOCOLATE
HAZELNUT torte

CHOCOLATE ALMOND
torte

RICH CHOCOLATE roulade

Roulade

- 8 ounces (250 g) bittersweet chocolate, coarsely chopped
- 8 large eggs, separated
- 1¼ cups (250 g) sugar
- ¼ teaspoon salt

Rich Chocolate Frosting

- 1 pound (500 g) bittersweet chocolate, coarsely chopped
- 1 cup (250 ml) heavy (double) cream
- 1 teaspoon vanilla extract (essence)
- 2 cups (300 g) confectioners' (icing) sugar

Serves 8–10 • Preparation 30 minutes + 30 minutes to chill • Cooking 25-35 minutes • Difficulty 2

Roulade

1. Preheat the oven to 350°F (180°C/gas 4). Butter a 10 x 15-inch (25 x 35-cm) jelly-roll pan. Line with parchment paper.

2. Melt the chocolate in a double boiler over barely simmering water, or in the microwave. Let cool.

3. Beat the egg yolks and sugar in a large bowl until pale and thick. Gradually beat in the chocolate. Beat the egg whites and salt in a large bowl until stiff peaks form. Fold into the chocolate mixture. Spoon the batter into the prepared pan.

4. Bake for about 20 minutes, until springy to the touch. Cool the cake in the pan for 5 minutes.

Frosting

1. Melt the chocolate, cream, and vanilla in a double boiler over barely simmering water. Stir in the confectioners' sugar. Chill for 30 minutes, until cooled and thickened.

2. Roll up the cake. Unroll the cake and spread with half the frosting. Reroll the cake and spread with the remaining frosting. Slice and serve.

CHILLED CHOCOLATE ORANGE cake

8   large eggs, chilled (straight from the refrigerator)

1   pound (500 g) dark chocolate, 70 percent cocoa

1   cup (250 g) butter

¼   cup (60 ml) Grand Marnier

1   cup (250 ml) heavy (double) cream

2   tablespoons confectioners' (icing) sugar

½   teaspoon vanilla extract (essence)

Fresh mandarin segments, to serve

Serves 8–12 • Preparation 30 minutes + 8–12 hours to chill • Cooking 45–50 minutes • Difficulty 2

1. Preheat the oven to 325°F (170°C/gas 3). Line an 8-inch (20-cm) springform pan with parchment paper. Butter the sides of the pan. Wrap the outsides of the pan in aluminum foil; it needs to be waterproof.

2. Beat the eggs in a bowl with an electric mixer on medium-high speed until doubled in volume, about 5 minutes.

3. Melt the chocolate and butter in a double boiler over barely simmering water. Remove from the heat and stir in the Grand Marnier.

4. Fold the egg mixture into the chocolate mixture. Spoon the batter into the prepared pan. Put the pan in a roasting dish. Fill the roasting dish with enough boiling water to come halfway up the sides of the springform pan.

5. Bake for 45–50 minutes, until a thin glazed crust is beginning to form on the surface. The center of the cake should still jiggle slightly. Remove from the water bath and place on a rack. Chill for at least 8 hours, or overnight.

6. Beat the cream with the confectioners' sugar and vanilla until thick. Slice the cake and serve with a dollop of cream and the mandarin.

This warm chocolate dessert is quick and easy to prepare. It is perfect for family dinners.

CHOCOLATE ALMOND torte

1/4	cup (60 g) salted butter
1 1/4	cups (250 g) sugar
5	large eggs
2 1/2	cups (250 g) almond meal
5	ounces (150 g) coarsely grated dark chocolate
	Fresh berries and whipped cream, to serve

Serve 6–8 • Preparation 15 minutes • Cooking 40–45 minutes
Difficulty 1

1. Preheat the oven to 350°F (180°C/gas 4). Grease a 10-inch (25-cm) baking pan and line with parchment paper.

2. Beat the butter and sugar in a bowl until pale and creamy. Beat in the egg yolks one at a time. Fold in the almonds, followed by the grated chocolate.

3. Beat the egg whites in a separate bowl until stiff then gently fold into the chocolate mixture.

4. Spoon the batter into the prepared pan. Bake for 40–45 minutes, until just firm.

5. Slice and serve warm with the berries and cream.

If you liked this recipe, you will love these as well.

CHOCOLATE PECAN torte

RICH CHOCOLATE roulade

CHILLED CHOCOLATE ORANGE cake

COCO MERINGUE torte

Meringue

6	large egg whites
$1^3/_4$	cups (350 g) superfine (caster) sugar
2	cups (250 g) shredded (desiccated) coconut, lightly toasted
$^1/_4$	cup (30 g) shaved coconut, lightly toasted, to decorate
1	cup (150 g) fresh whole strawberries, to decorate

Strawberry Cream

2	cups (500 ml) heavy (double) cream
4	tablespoons confectioners' (icing) sugar
1	tablespoon kirsch (clear cherry brandy)
$^1/_2$	teaspoon ground cinnamon
$3^1/_2$	ounces (100 g) white chocolate, melted and cooled
$1^1/_2$	cups (250 g) fresh strawberries, chopped

Serves 6–8 • Preparation 30 minutes • Cooking 1 hour • Difficulty 2

Meringue

1. Preheat the oven to 275°F (140°C/gas 1). Line four 17 x 14-inch (43 x 35-cm) baking sheets with parchment paper and mark with 9-inch (23-cm) circles.

2. Beat the egg whites in a bowl with an electric mixer on medium speed until soft peaks form. Gradually add the sugar, beating until thick and glossy. Fold in the coconut. Spoon the meringue onto the circles on the prepared baking sheets and spread to fill.

3. Bake for 1 hour, until crisp. Remove from the oven, let cool for 10 minutes. Place on wire racks to cool completely.

Strawberry Cream

1. Beat the cream and sugar until soft peaks form. Fold in the kirsch, cinnamon, chocolate, and chopped strawberries.

2. To assemble, spread a quarter of the strawberry cream on each meringue disk. Sandwich the disks together into one tall layer cake. Arrange the whole strawberries and shaved coconut decoratively on the top layer. Slice and serve.

PAVLOVA with fresh berries

Meringue
4	large egg whites
	Pinch of salt
1	cup (200 g) superfine (caster) sugar
1	tablespoon cornstarch (corn flour)
1	teaspoon white vinegar
1	teaspoon vanilla extract (essence)

Topping
1¼	cups (310 ml) heavy (double) cream
2	cups (300 g) strawberries, halved
1	cup (150 g) raspberries
1	cup (150 g) blueberries

Serves 6–8 • Preparation 30 minutes • Cooking 1¼–1½ hours • Difficulty 2

Meringue

1. Preheat the oven to 300°F (150°C/gas 2). Grease a large baking sheet. Draw an 8-inch (20-cm) disk on a piece of parchment paper and place disk-side down on the prepared sheet.

2. Beat the egg whites and salt in a bowl with an electric mixer on medium speed until soft peaks form. Gradually add the sugar, beating until the meringue is thick and glossy and the sugar has completely dissolved. Add the cornstarch, vinegar, and vanilla and beat to combine.

3. Spoon the meringue into the center of the marked disk and spread out to an even thickness. Sweep a spatula up the sides to create decorative waves.

4. Put the pavlova in the oven and decrease the temperature to 250°F (130°C/gas ½). Bake for 1¼–1½ hours, until just crisp on the outside, but not colored. Turn the oven off and leave with the door ajar until cooled completely.

Topping

1. Beat the cream in a bowl with an electric mixer on medium speed until stiff peaks form. Spread over the pavlova and sprinkle with the berries. Slice and serve.

This is a very handsome dessert cake. It is perfect for special occasions.

LEMON cheesecake

Crust

1½ cups (150 g) almond meal

¼ cup (50 g) brown sugar

¼ cup (60 g) melted salted butter

Filling

1½ pounds (750 g) cream cheese, at room temperature

3 large eggs

1 cup (200 g) sugar

2 teaspoons vanilla extract (essence)

3 tablespoons freshly squeezed lemon juice

1 tablespoon finely grated unwaxed lemon zest

Topping

2 cups (500 ml) sour cream

¼ cup (50 g) sugar

Glaze

½ cup (100 g) sugar

2 tablespoons cornstarch (cornflour)

½ cup (120 ml) water

⅓ cup (90 ml) freshly squeezed lemon juice

Serves 12 • Preparation 1 hour + 12 hours to chill • Cooking 50-60 minutes • Difficulty 3

Crust

1. Preheat the oven to 350°F (180°C/gas 4).

2. Mix the almond meal, brown sugar, and butter in a bowl. Press the mixture into the bottom of a 10-inch (25-cm) springform pan. Bake for 8–10 minutes, until crisp. Set aside on a wire rack to cool.

Filling

1. Beat the cream cheese in a bowl until smooth. Add the eggs one at a time, beating until smooth after each addition. Gradually add the sugar, beating until smooth. Beat in the lemon juice, vanilla, and lemon zest.

2. Spoon the filling over the crust and bake for 30–35 minutes, until set but not browned.

3. Stir the sour cream and sugar in a bowl. Remove the cheesecake from the oven and carefully spread the sour cream mixture over the top. Bake for 12–15 more minutes.

4. Let cool on a wire rack for 30 minutes. Transfer to the refrigerator and chill for about one hour, until the topping is cool, but not completely chilled.

Glaze

1. Mix the sugar and cornstarch in a small saucepan. Whisk in the water and lemon juice. Bring to a boil, whisking constantly until thickened. Cook 1 minute and then let cool.

2. Pour the cooled glaze over the cool cheesecake and spread to cover completely. Chill overnight before serving.

FRESH FRUIT with vermouth

Serves 4 • Preparation 15 minutes + 1 hour to chill
Difficulty 1

2	oranges	1/4	teaspoon ground cinnamon + extra, to dust
1	pink grapefruit		
2	bananas, thinly sliced		
2	kiwifruit, thinly sliced	1/2	cup (120 ml) sweet white vermouth
	Freshly squeezed juice of 1/2 lemon		Whipped cream or Greek-style yogurt, to serve
4	tablespoons dark brown sugar		

1. Peel the oranges and grapefruit and chop into small pieces. Place in a medium bowl. Mix with the sliced bananas and kiwifruit.

2. Add the lemon juice, brown sugar, cinnamon, and vermouth. Refrigerate for at least 1 hour.

3. Spoon the salad into four serving glasses or bowls. Dust with a little extra cinnamon and serve with the whipped cream or yogurt.

ZABAGLIONE with berries

Serves 4–6 • Preparation 10 minutes + 2 hours to chill
Cooking 10–15 minutes • Difficulty 2

4	large egg yolks	2	cups (300 g) fresh strawberries, sliced
4	tablespoons sugar		
1/2	cup (120 ml) dry Marsala wine		Finely chopped toasted nuts, to sprinkle

1. Beat the egg yolks and sugar in the top pot of a double boiler with an electric mixer at high speed until pale and creamy. Gradually beat in the Marsala.

2. Place over barely simmering water and simmer, stirring constantly with a wooden spoon, until thick, 10–15 minutes. Remove from the heat and transfer to a bowl.

3. Cover the bowl and chill in the refrigerator for 2 hours.

4. To prepare the desserts, divide the strawberries evenly among six dessert glasses or bowls. Spoon the chilled zabaglione over the top. Sprinkle with the nuts, and serve.

CHOCOLATE mousse

Serves 4 • Preparation 15 minutes + 2–12 hours to chill
Cooking 2–3 minutes • Difficulty 2

4	large egg yolks		+ extra curls, to decorate
1/4	cup (50 g) firmly packed light brown sugar	2	tablespoons unsweetened cocoa powder
1/8	teaspoon salt		
2	ounces (60 g) dark chocolate, finely chopped	3/4	cup (180 ml) heavy (double) cream

1. Whisk the egg yolks, brown sugar, and salt in a double boiler over barely simmering water until the sugar is dissolved and mixture is warm, 2–3 minutes.

2. Remove from the heat and whisk in the finely chopped chocolate and cocoa until melted and smooth. Let cool to room temperature.

3. Beat the cream in a medium bowl with an electric mixer on medium speed until soft peaks form. Stir half of the whipped cream into the chocolate mixture. Gently fold in the remaining whipped cream.

4. Divide the mousse evenly among four serving glasses or bowls. Cover and chill 2–12 hours.

5. Remove the mousses from the refrigerator 15 minutes before serving. Garnish with the chocolate curls and serve.

PANNA COTTA & choco sauce

Serves 6 • Preparation 30 minutes + 4 hours to chill
Cooking 5 minutes • Difficulty 2

Panna Cotta

2	cups (500 ml) heavy (double) cream	2–3	tablespoons peach brandy
2/3	cup (150 ml) milk	1/4	cup (60 ml) cold water
1/3	cup (75 g) sugar	1	heaped tablespoon unflavored gelatin
2	teaspoons vanilla extract (essence)		

Chocolate Sauce

4	ounces (120 g) dark chocolate

Panna Cotta

1. Beat the cream, milk, sugar, vanilla, and brandy in a saucepan over medium heat until almost boiling.

2. Put the cold water in a bowl and sprinkle with the gelatin. Leave to stand for 5 minutes to soften.

3. Remove the cream mixture from the heat and use a whisk to beat in the gelatin until dissolved. Pour into six small ramekins or molds and set aside to cool.

4. Cover and chill for at least 4 hours before serving.

Chocolate Sauce

1. Melt the chocolate in a double boiler over barely simmering water. Let cool a little.

2. Unmold the panna cottas and spoon the warm chocolate sauce over the top. Serve at once.

"Crisp" is the American term for what the British call a "crumble." To vary this recipe, use six apples and 2 cups (300 g) of fresh blackberries.

APPLE crisp

Apple Mixture

8	medium apples (about 2 pounds/1 kg), peeled, cored and chopped
1	tablespoons freshly squeezed lemon juice
1/3	cup (70 g) sugar
1	tablespoon cornstarch (cornflour)
1/2	teaspoon ground cinnamon
1/2	teaspoon ground ginger
1/4	teaspoon ground nutmeg
	Pinch of sea salt flakes

Topping

1/2	cup (100 g) firmly packed light brown sugar
1/4	cup (30 g) gluten-free flour mix
1/2	cup (50 g) gluten-free rolled oats
1/4	cup (25 g) almond meal
1/2	teaspoon cinnamon
1/2	teaspoon sea salt flakes
1/3	cup (90 g) melted unsalted butter

To Serve

Whipped cream or vanilla ice cream

Serves 4-6 • Preparation 20 minutes + 10-15 minutes to rest • Cooking 50-60 minutes • Difficulty 1

Apple Mixture

1. Preheat the oven to 375°F (180°C/gas 5). Lightly butter a 9-inch (23-cm) square baking dish.

2. Put the apples in a bowl and drizzle with lemon juice. Toss with the sugar, cornstarch, cinnamon, ginger, nutmeg, and salt. Spread out evenly in the prepared baking dish.

Topping

1. Combine the brown sugar, flour, oats, almond meal, cinnamon, salt, and melted butter in a bowl, mixing well. Sprinkle over the apples in the baking dish

2. Bake for 50-60 minutes, until the apples are soft and the topping is golden brown.

3. Let rest 10-15 minutes before serving. Serve warm with ice cream or whipped cream.

If you liked this recipe, you will love these as well.

FRESH FRUIT
with vermouth

ZABAGLIONE
with berries

EASY ICE CREAM
cake

FROZEN RICOTTA cake

1 pound (500 g) fresh ricotta cheese, strained

$\frac{1}{2}$ cup (60 g) walnuts, chopped

$\frac{1}{2}$ cup (60 g) pistachios, chopped

$\frac{1}{2}$ cup (60 g) dark chocolate, chopped

$\frac{1}{2}$ cup (50 g) mixed candied (glacé) fruit, chopped

$\frac{1}{2}$ cup (60 g) raisins

$\frac{1}{2}$ cup (100 g) sugar

2 tablespoons kirsch (or other fruit liqueur)

1 tablespoon finely grated unwaxed lemon zest

1 tablespoon finely grated unwaxed orange zest

1 teaspoon vanilla extract (essence)

Serves 4–6 • Preparation 15 minutes + 6–12 hours to freeze • Difficulty 1

1. Line a 5 x 9-inch (12 x 23-cm) loaf pan with aluminum foil, letting the edges overhang.

2. Combine the ricotta, walnuts, pistachios, chocolate, candied fruit, raisins, sugar, liqueur, lemon and orange zest, and vanilla in a large bowl and mix well. Spoon the mixture into the prepared pan. Freeze for at 6 hours, or overnight.

3. Turn out onto a serving dish and carefully remove the foil. Slice and serve.

EASY ICE CREAM cake

1   quart (1 liter) chocolate ice cream, softened

1   quart (1 liter) strawberry ice cream, softened

2   cups (500 ml) heavy (double) cream

2   tablespoons confectioners' (icing) sugar

1   teaspoon vanilla extract (essence)

1   cup (150 g) strawberries, sliced

3   kiwifruit, peeled and sliced

Serves 6–8 • Preparation 25 minutes + 4–12 hours to freeze • Difficulty 1

1. Line a 10-inch (25-cm) springform pan with aluminum foil.

2. Spoon the chocolate ice cream into the prepared pan, followed by the strawberry ice cream. Cover with aluminum foil and freeze for 2 hours, or overnight.

3. Beat the cream, confectioners' sugar, and vanilla in a large bowl with an electric mixer at high speed until stiff.

4. Loosen and remove the pan sides. Turn the ice cream cake out onto a serving plate.

5. Decorate with the cream and fresh fruit, and serve.

This frozen meringue cake is based on an old Italian recipe. It makes an impressive finish to any meal. It can also be prepared with 1 quart (1 liter) each of two commercially-made ice creams. Choose your favorite flavors to combine. If using commercially-made ice-cream, check that it is gluten-free.

CHOCOLATE NOUGAT semifreddo

Meringue
$1/2$ cup (75 g) confectioners' (icing) sugar
2 large egg whites

Nougat Gelato
1 cup (250 ml) milk
1 cup (250 ml) heavy (double) cream
$3/4$ cup (150 g) sugar
1 tablespoon cognac
2 ounces (60 g) firm nougat, finely chopped

Chocolate Gelato
2 cups (500 ml) milk
1 vanilla pod, sliced open lengthwise
4 large egg yolks
$3/4$ cup (150 g) sugar
4 ounces (120 g) dark chocolate, chopped

Topping
2 cups (500 ml) heavy (double) cream
Dark chocolate, grated, to decorate

Serves 10–12 • Preparation 1 hour + time to churn & 2 hours to freeze
Cooking $1^1/2$ hours • Difficulty 2

Meringue

1. Preheat the oven to 200°F (95°C). Line a baking sheet with parchment paper. Use the base of a 12-inch (30-cm) springform pan to trace a circle on the paper.

2. Beat the egg whites in a bowl until stiff. Add the sugar gradually, beating until thick and glossy.

3. Spoon the meringue onto the disk. Bake until dry, about $1^1/2$ hours. Remove from the oven and let cool.

Nougat Gelato

1. Stir the milk, cream, and sugar in a saucepan over medium heat until the sugar has dissolved. Let cool. Add the cognac. Transfer to an ice-cream machine and churn following the manufacturer's instructions. When almost frozen add the nougat. Place the gelato in the freezer.

Chocolate Gelato

1. Bring the milk and vanilla pod to a boil in a saucepan. Beat the egg yolks and sugar in a bowl until pale and creamy. Gradually add the milk mixture. Discard the vanilla pod. Return the mixture to the pan. Stir over low heat until it coats the spoon. Stir in the chocolate and let cool. Transfer to an ice-cream machine and churn. Freeze.

2. Line a 12-inch (30-cm) springform pan with parchment paper. Let both gelatos stand at room temperature for 10 minutes. Spread the nougat gelato in the pan. Top with the chocolate gelato and the meringue disk. Freeze for 2 hours.

3. Beat the cream in a bowl until thick. Unmold the torte and decorate with the cream. Sprinkle with chocolate and serve.

INDEX